# Problem-Solving

## TABLE OF CONTENTS  6B

# UNIT 1  Units of Measure

## EXAMPLE

Bill is painting a box which is 130 mm long, 5 cm wide and 1 dm high.  How many square metres does he have to paint?

Think :   130 mm = 13 cm = 0.13 m ; 5 cm = 0.05 m ; 1dm = 0.1 m

Write :   Areas of 2 sides : $0.13 \times 0.1 \times 2 = 0.026$

Areas of 2 ends : $0.1 \times 0.05 \times 2 = 0.01$

Areas of top and bottom : $0.13 \times 0.05 \times 2 = 0.013$

Total areas : $0.026 + 0.01 + 0.013 = 0.049$

*Answer :*   He has to paint 0.049 m$^2$.

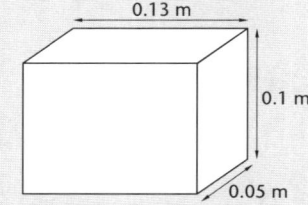

## Complete the tables and solve the problems.  Show your work.

①

| m | 40 | | | | 950 | |
|---|---|---|---|---|---|---|
| cm | | 200 | | 80 000 | | |
| km | | | 4.5 | | | 0.7 |

②

| g | 900 | | 50 | | 60 000 | |
|---|---|---|---|---|---|---|
| kg | | 8.3 | | 0.29 | | 3.44 |

③

| mL | | 450 | | 52 000 | | 9 |
|---|---|---|---|---|---|---|
| L | 2.05 | | 0.11 | | 32.4 | |

④   State True or False for each of the following.

   a.   40 cm + 8 dm = 840 cm

   b.   500 mm + 6 m = 650 cm

   c.   8.2 kg + 200 g = 8400 g

   d.   0.5 L + 400 mL = 0.54 L

> • *Length :*   1 km = 1000 m  ← **Read this first.**
>              1 m = 10 dm
>              1 dm = 10 cm
>              1 cm = 10 mm
> • *Weight :*   1 kg = 1000 g
> • *Capacity :* 1 L = 1000 mL

*Answer :* a. _____ b. _____ c. _____ d. _____

Kelly and Milly were buying candies and drinks for their party.

⑤ Kelly bought 1.3 kg of jellybeans and 250 g of cinnamon hearts. How many grams of candies did she buy in all?

Answer : _____

⑥ Milly wanted to buy some licorice that was priced per 100g. If she wanted to buy 0.75 kg of licorice, how many times the price per 100 g would she pay?

Answer : _____

⑦ They wanted to buy some small bags to put the candies in and ribbons to tie them up. If they bought 14 cm of red ribbon, 0.8 m of blue ribbon and 1200 mm of white ribbon, how many metres of ribbon did they buy?

Answer : _____

⑧ How many centimetres of ribbon did they buy?

Answer : _____

⑨ Milly bought 2 bags of candies. They weighed 1.03 kg and 800 g. How many kilograms of candies did she buy in all?

Answer : _____

⑩ On average, each bag weighed 600 g. If the total weight of bags was 2.4 kg, how many bags of candies did they buy in all?

Answer : _____

⑪ If the total amount of juice in 5 containers was 2.25 L, how many millilitres of juice did 1 container hold on average?

Answer : _____

⑫ Container A could hold 0.89 L of juice and container B could hold 450 mL of juice. How much more juice in litres could container A hold than container B?

Answer : _____

# CHALLENGE

Freda was piling tiles. Each tile was 8 mm thick and weighed 18 g.

① How many tiles were there in a pile of 6.4 m high?

Answer : _____

② How many kilograms did the 6.4 m high pile of tiles weigh?

Answer : _____

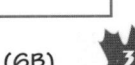

# Operations with Money

## EXAMPLE

Billy bought 2 boxes of chocolates for $12.70 each. The cashier charged him an additional $3.81 for taxes. What was his change from a $50 bill?

Total cost : $12.7 \times 2 + 3.81 = 29.21$

Change : $50 - 29.21 = 20.79$

*Answer :* His change was $20.79.

## Solve the problems. Show your work.

Milly and Jeffrey went shopping at their favourite mall. All the purchases were tax free that day.

① Milly was looking for a blouse. Store A had the blouse on sale for $35.98. Store B had the same blouse on sale for $41.52, but offered her a $5.25 discount. Which store had the lower price?

*Answer :* Store _____ had the lower price. _____

② If Milly bought the cheaper blouse and the cashier gave the change to her with the fewest coins or bills, what was her change from a $50 bill? What were the coins or bills?

*Answer :* _____

③ Milly wanted to buy some candies. She saw her favourite candy on sale for $1.49 per 100 g. How much would it cost her for 0.7 kg?

*Answer :* _____

④ If the cashier gave the change to her with the fewest coins, what was her change from a $10 bill and a twoonie? What were the coins?

*Answer :* _____

⑤    Jeffrey wanted to buy some shoe polish for his old boots. Store C had it on sale for $3.95 for a 125-g tube, but store D sold it for $2.99 for a 100-g jar. Which was a better buy?

*Answer :* _____

⑥    Jeffrey wanted to call his friend, but he did not have any quarters. If he changed his $10 bill into quarters, how many quarters would he get?

*Answer :* _____

⑦    In the food court, hamburgers were sold for $2.49 each, French Fries for $1.39 each and soft drinks for $1.25 each. If Jeffrey bought 2 hamburgers and 1 soft drink and paid with the fewest number of coins, what coins would he pay for his food?

*Answer :* _____

⑧    Milly used one-eighth of her money to buy 1 hamburger, 1 order of French Fries and 1 soft drink. How much money did Milly have at the beginning?

*Answer :* _____

⑨    Milly bought 4 boxes of chocolates for $11.16. She opened 1 box and found that the chocolates did not taste good. Then Milly returned 3 boxes of chocolates. How much money did Milly get back?

*Answer :* _____

⑩    The average cost of 2 bags of popcorn and a jumbo soft drink was $4.32. If the average cost of 2 bags of popcorn was $4.59, how much did the jumbo soft drink cost?

*Answer :* _____

⑪    Jeffrey had 4 quarters, 24 dimes and 16 nickels left. Did he have enough money to buy a jumbo soft drink? Explain.

*Answer :* _____

Jerry got a part-time job in Alco Parking Lot. He wanted to save some money for a trip in summer.

⑫ If he got paid $7.05 per hour and worked 18 hours a week, how much could he earn per week?

_Answer :_ _____

⑬ Jerry worked 6 days a week and took a bus to and from work. If the bus fare was $1.85 per trip, how much did he earn each week after paying for the transportation?

_Answer :_ _____

⑭ Jerry's employer deducted $25.38 of his weekly earnings for income tax. How much did he earn after paying for transportation and the deduction?

_Answer :_ _____

⑮ Jerry wanted to save up at least $600.00 for the trip. How many weeks would he have to work to save this amount?

_Answer :_ _____

⑯ In the parking lot, the parking fee for the 1st half hour was $1.75 and $3.00 for every extra half hour. How much was the parking fee for 2 hours and 25 minutes?

_Answer :_ _____

⑰ Mr Keller parked his car for 1 hour and 46 minutes. Jerry gave $1.25 change to him. How much did Mr Keller give to Jerry for his parking fee?

_Answer :_ _____

⑱ Jerry had to prepare some coins for change. If he traded a $5 bill for nickels, how many nickels would he get?

_Answer :_ _____

Jerry recorded the money collected in the past 6 days. Use his table to write the amount of money in words to complete what he said.

| Day | Mon | Tue | Wed | Thu | Fri | Sat |
| --- | --- | --- | --- | --- | --- | --- |
| Money Collected ($) | 5975.45 | 6094.00 | 4210.30 | 3981.95 | 5700.40 | 9008.10 |

- *It is easier to know the values of decimal numbers if we place them on a place value chart.*

*e.g. 2736.54*

Read this first.

| Thousands | | | | | | Tenths | Hun-dredths |
| --- | --- | --- | --- | --- | --- | --- | --- |
| H | T | O | H | T | O | | |
| | | | 2 | 7 | 3 | 6. 5 | 4 |

It's busy working here. Last week, I collected :

⑲ _____ on Monday,

⑳ _____ on Tuesday,

㉑ _____ on Wednesday,

㉒ _____ on Thursday,

㉓ _____ on Friday, and

㉔ _____ on Saturday.

# CHALLENGE

Gary had 50 coins. $\frac{1}{2}$ of his coins were twoonies, $\frac{1}{10}$ loonies, $\frac{1}{5}$ quarters, $\frac{1}{10}$ dimes and the rest nickels. How much did Gary have? Did he have enough money to trade for a $50 bill?

| | Twoonie | Loonie | Quarter | Dime | Nickel |
| --- | --- | --- | --- | --- | --- |
| No. of coins | | | | | |

*Answer :*

## E X A M P L E

Tommy left home at 10:42 a.m. and walked to the mall, a distance of 2 km. If Tommy arrived at the mall at 11:07 a.m., how long did he take to walk there? What was his walking speed?

Time taken :    11 h 07 min – 10 h 42 min = 25 min

Speed :   2 ÷ 25 = 0.08

*Answer :*    He took 25 min to walk to the mall.
His walking speed was 0.08 km/min.

## Solve the problems.  Show your work.

Sandy, Elaine and Matthew were going on a car trip.  They were going to meet at Elaine's house.  Sandy's house was 1040 m from Elaine's house and Matthew's house was 2160 m from Elaine's house.

① If Sandy walked at an average speed of 0.08 km/min, how long would it take her to reach Elaine's house?

*Answer :*  It would take her _____ .

② Matthew had to arrive at Elaine's house at 11:00 a.m.  If Matthew left his house at 10:42 a.m., at what speed should he walk so as to reach Elaine's house on time?

*Answer :* _____

③ If Matthew's speed was also 0.08 km/min, at what time would he reach Elaine's house?

*Answer :* _____

④ The first part of their trip was 506 km long.  It took them 9.2 hours to drive there.  What was their average speed?

*Answer :* _____

⑤ The three friends took turns driving. If Sandy drove 2 hours 45 minutes and Elaine drove 3 hours 30 minutes, how long did Matthew drive?

*Answer :* _____

⑥ The next day, they drove at an average speed of 72 km/h for 6 hours and 50 km/h for 1 hour 33 minutes.  How far did they drive in all?

*Answer :* _____

⑦ On the third day, they drove 300 km in 3 hours 12 minutes. What was their average speed in kilometres per hour?

*Answer :* _____

⑧ Sandy drove at 60 km/h to the convenience store 36 km away and returned to the motel at 40 km/h. If she left the motel at 12:44 p.m., at what time did she return?

*Answer :* _____

⑨ On the fourth day, they visited a museum which was 138.92 km from the motel. They left the motel at 2:45 p.m. and took 2 hours and 18 minutes to reach there. At what time did they reach the museum?

*Answer :* _____

⑩ What was their average speed in kilometres per hour?

*Answer :* _____

⑪ If they wanted to reach the museum 16 min earlier than their actual arrival time, what time would it be?

*Answer :* _____

⑫ At what speed would they have to drive then? (correct to 2 decimal places)

*Answer :* _____

# CHALLENGE

A car started from Townville at an average speed of 80 km/h towards Littleton. A truck started from Littleton at an average speed of 50 km/h towards Townville. If both the car and the truck started at 2:45 p.m. and passed each other at 6:15 p.m., what was the distance between Townville and Littleton?

*Answer :* _____

# Perimeter and Area

## EXAMPLE

Rose wanted to plant a herb garden in the shape of a triangle as shown. How much edging would she need to go all the way around the garden? What was the area of the garden?

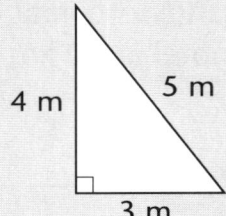

Perimeter :  5 + 4 + 3 = 12

Area :  3 × 4 ÷ 2 = 6

*Answer :*  Rose would need 12 m of edging. The area of the garden was 6 m².

## Look at the pieces of cardboard and solve the problems. Show your work.

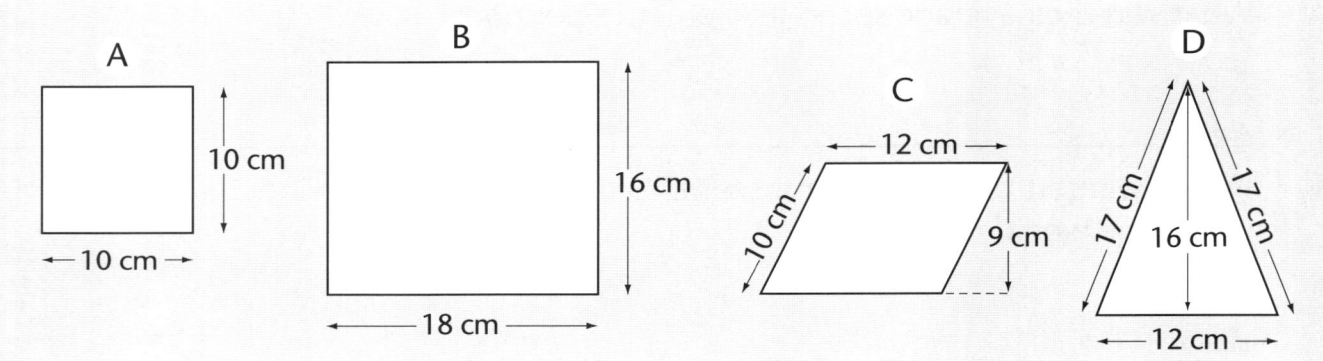

① Olive wanted to decorate the edges of each piece of cardboard with a braid border. How long would the braid border be for A?

*Answer :* Her braid border would be _____ long.

② How long would the braid border be for B?

*Answer :* _____

③ How long would the braid border be for C?

*Answer :* _____

④ How long would the braid border be for D?

*Answer :* _____

⑤ What was the area of A?

Answer : _____

⑥ What was the area of B?

Answer : _____

⑦ What was the area of C?

Answer : _____

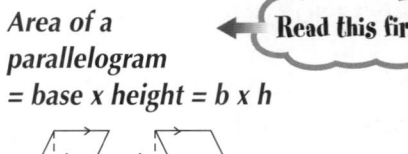
Area of a parallelogram
= base x height = b x h

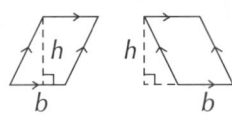

Area of a triangle
= $\frac{1}{2}$ base x height = $\frac{1}{2}$ b x h

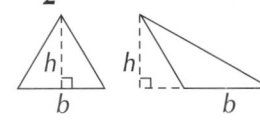

⑧ What was the area of D?

Answer : _____

⑨ Olive cut out a square from the middle of A, leaving 2 cm on each side. What was the area of the cardboard left?

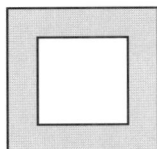

Answer : _____

⑩ Olive cut out a rectangle from the middle of B, again leaving 2 cm on each side. What was the area of the cardboard left?

Answer : _____

⑪ Olive cut out a parallelogram from the middle of C as shown.

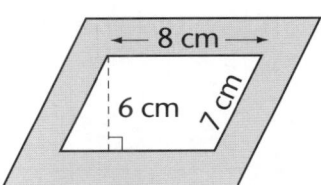

a. What was the area of the cardboard left?

Answer : _____

b. What was the perimeter of the cutout part?

Answer : _____

⑫ Olive cut out a triangle from the middle of D. What was the area of the cardboard left?

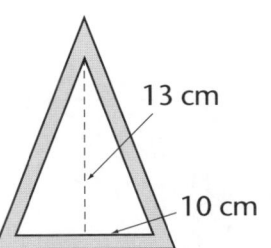

Answer : _____

## Solve the problems. Show your work.

Lori had a design project for school. She had to design a house for the future.

⑬ Lori wanted to have a rectangular living room which had 180 m² of space. If its length was 15 m long, what was its width?

Answer : _____

⑭ If all the ceilings were 3 m high, how much wallpaper would be needed to cover all the walls of the living room? (Ignore the windows and doors.)

Answer : _____

⑮ Lori wanted to carpet the living room, leaving a 1-m border of hardwood all the way around the room. How much carpeting would she need?

Answer : _____

⑯ Lori's kitchen was in the shape of a triangle as shown. What was the perimeter of her kitchen?

Lori's kitchen

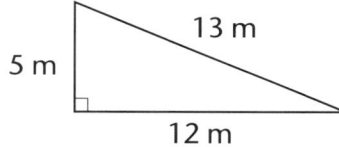

Answer : _____

⑰ How many square metres of tiles would Lori need to cover the kitchen?

Answer : _____

⑱ If 1 can of paint could cover 5 m² and Lori wanted to paint the walls of the kitchen, how many cans of paint would Lori need? (Ignore the windows and doors.)

Answer : _____

⑲ The bedroom was going to be in the shape of a parallelogram, 18 m long and 16 m high. How much carpeting would Lori need to cover the floor area?

Answer : _____

Each small square has an area of 1 cm². Sketch the shapes and solve the problems.

⑳ A square with an area of 36 cm².

㉓ A triangle with an area of 18 cm².

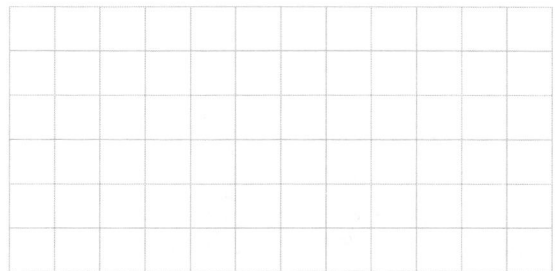

㉔ Lori said, 'I can make different parallelograms, each with an area of 24 cm² and a base of 6 cm.' Draw 3 different parallelograms in the box to show that what Lori said is correct.

㉑ A rectangle with an area of 24 cm² and a perimeter of 22 cm.

㉒ A parallelogram with an area of 36 cm².

㉕ Tim said, 'I can make different triangles, each with an area of 18 cm² and a base of 6 cm.' Draw 3 different triangles in the box to show that what Tim said is correct.

# CHALLENGE

① What is the perimeter of the shaded part?

Answer : _____

② What is the area of the shaded part?

Answer : _____

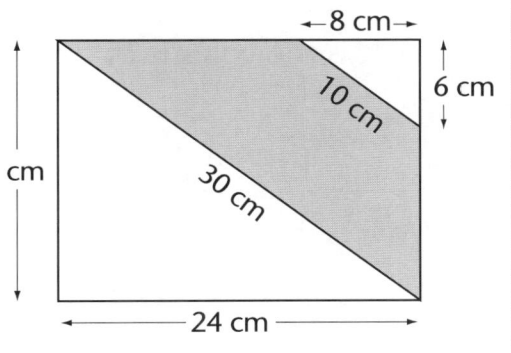

# Volume

## EXAMPLE

When Dylan put a stone into a rectangular aquarium 50 cm long and 30 cm wide, the water level rose 5 cm. What was the volume of the stone?

Think :     Volume of a rectangular prism
           = Surface area of the base × height

           Volume of the stone
           = Volume of the water displaced

Volume :   (50 × 30) × 5 = 7500

*Answer :*     The volume of the stone was 7500 cm³.

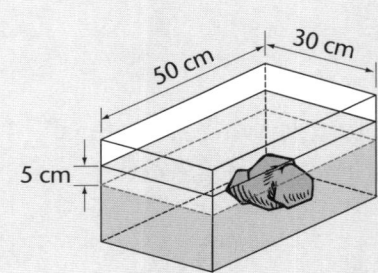

## Solve the problems.  Show your work.

Gary wants to find the volume of each brick.  He puts each of them in a container with 200 mL of water.

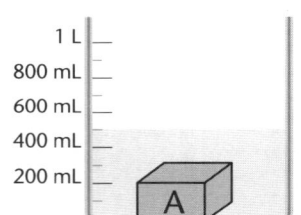   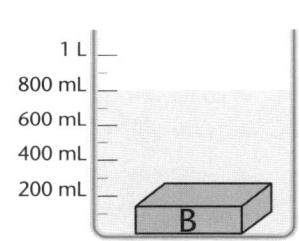   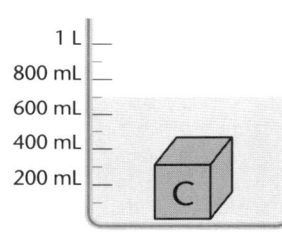   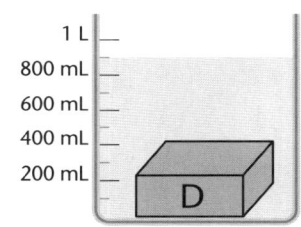

①  What is the volume of brick A?


*Answer :*  The volume is _____ .

②  What is the volume of brick B?


*Answer :* _____

③  What is the volume of brick C?


*Answer :* _____

④  What is the volume of brick D?


*Answer :* _____

⑤  List the bricks in order from the one with the greatest volume to the least.


*Answer :* _____

⑥  If brick A is 5 cm high, what is the area of its base?


*Answer :* _____

⑦  If brick A is 6 cm wide, what is its length?


*Answer :* _____

⑧ If brick B is 6 cm high, what is the area of its base?

*Answer :* _____

⑨ If brick B is 25 cm long, what is its width?

*Answer :* _____

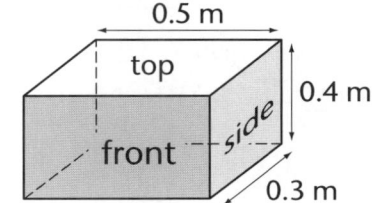

**Don't forget** ← **Read this first.**

$1 \ cm^3 = 1 \ mL$
$1000 \ cm^3 = 1000 \ mL = 1 \ L$

area of base

*Volume of a rectangular prism*
height

= area of base x height = length x width x height

⑩ If the area of the base of brick D is 140 cm², what is its height?

*Answer :* _____

⑪ Gary wants to pack as many A bricks as he can into the transparent container on the right. Draw the top, front and side view of the container in the space below to show how many A bricks you can see.

0.5 m
top
0.4 m
front — side
0.3 m

| Top view | Side view | Front view |
|----------|-----------|------------|
|          |           |            |

⑫ How many layers of bricks are there in the container ? How many bricks are in each layer?

*Answer :* _____

⑬ How many bricks can be put in the container?

*Answer :* _____

⑭ How many litres of water can the container hold?

*Answer :* _____

Dolores has a plastic box in the shape of a rectangular prism. Its base area is 120 cm$^2$ and its volume is 1500 cm$^3$.

⑮ The length of the box is 15 cm. What is its width?

Answer : _____

⑯ What is the height of the box?

Answer : _____

⑰ How many litres of water can the box hold?

Answer : _____

⑱ Dolores is going to use her box to fill two containers with sand. Container A is a rectangular prism 0.5 m long, 0.45 m wide and 0.2 m high. What is its volume?

Answer : _____

⑲ How many boxes of sand does Dolores need to fill up container A?

Answer : _____

⑳ Dolores uses 40 boxes of sand to fill up container B. What is the volume of container B?

Answer : _____

㉑ If the height of container B is 60 cm, what is its base area?

Answer : _____

㉒ If Dolores empties the sand in container A into container B, how high will the sand reach?

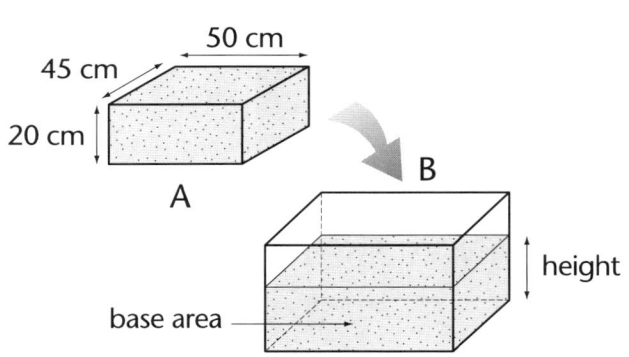

Answer : _____

Jillian lives in a condominium where there is a huge swimming pool.

㉓ The swimming pool is 30 m long, 21 m wide and 1.8 m deep. What is the volume of the pool?

*Answer :* _____

㉔ How many litres of water can the swimming pool hold?

$1\ m^3 = 1\ 000\ 000\ cm^3$

$1000\ cm^3 = 1\ L$

$1\ m^3 = (1\ 000\ 000 \div 1000)\ L$
   $= 1000\ L$

*e.g.*   $15\ 000\ L$
   $= (15\ 000 \div 1000)\ m^3$
   $= 15\ m^3$

*Read this first.*

*Answer :* _____

㉕ If the swimming pool is filled to a depth of 1.6 m, how many litres of water will there be?

㉗ If 30 000 L of water is pumped into the swimming pool each hour, how long will it take to fill up the entire swimming pool?

*Answer :* _____

*Answer :* _____

㉖ How much water should be pumped into the swimming pool to raise the water level from 1.6 m to 1.7 m?

㉘ If 126 000 L of water is pumped into the swimming pool, how much will the water level rise?

*Answer :* _____

*Answer :* _____

# CHALLENGE

What is the volume of the solid on the right?

*Answer :* _____

# Two- and Three-Dimensional Figures

## EXAMPLE

Marci says, 'These 2 triangles are congruent.' Is he correct? Explain.

Think : Method 1 – Trace and cut out one of the figures. Then flip, slide or turn the cutout to see if it matches the other figure. If the 2 figures match, they are congruent.

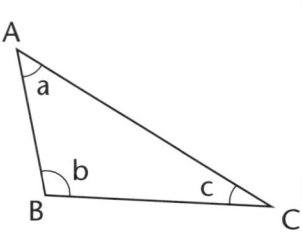

Method 2 – Measure the corresponding sides and angles. If they are equal, the figures are congruent.

AB = PQ = 2cm ; BC = QR = 3 cm ;
AC = PR = 4 cm ;

a = p = 47˚ ; b = q = 105˚ ; c = r = 28˚

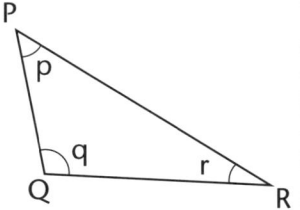

Answer : Marci is correct because the corresponding sides and angles of the 2 triangles are equal.

**Donny has drawn 4 triangles. Measure the triangles to complete the table. Then solve the problems.**

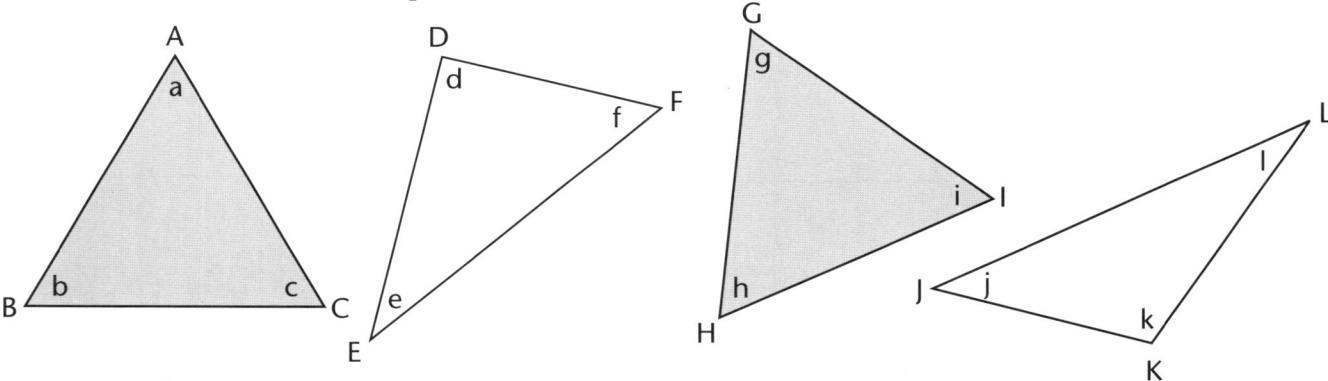

| | Triangle | Side | | | Angle | | |
|---|---|---|---|---|---|---|---|
| ① | ABC | AB = | BC = | CA = | a = | b = | c = |
| ② | DEF | DE = | EF = | FD = | d = | e = | f = |
| ③ | GHI | GH= | HI = | IG = | g = | h = | i = |
| ④ | JKL | JK = | KL = | LJ = | j = | k = | l = |

⑤ Which 2 triangles are congruent? Explain.

Answer : _____

⑥ Which triangles are acute triangles?

Answer : _____

⑦ Which triangle is a right triangle?

Answer : _____

⑧ Which triangle is an obtuse triangle?

Answer : _____

⑨ Which triangles are equilateral triangles?

Answer : _____

⑩ Which triangles are scalene triangles?

Answer : _____

⑪ Construct an acute scalene triangle in the box.

**Donny has made 4 solids.  Name the solids and complete the table.  Solve the problems.**

| | | Name | No. of vertices | No. of faces | No. of edges |
|---|---|---|---|---|---|
| ⑫ | A | | | | |
| ⑬ | B | | | | |
| ⑭ | C | | | | |
| ⑮ | D | | | | |

⑯ Draw the top view and side view of solid B.

| Top view | Side view |
|---|---|
| | |

⑰ Draw the top view and side view of solid C.

| Top view | Side view |
|---|---|
| | |

## Draw the missing face of each net.  Then solve the problems.

⑱  a.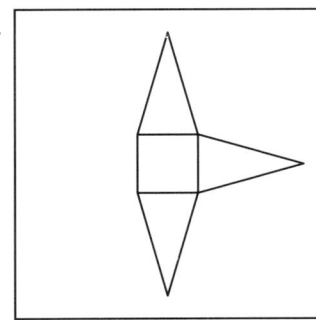

b. What is the solid that can be made from this net?

Answer : _____

c. How many triangular faces does this solid have?

Answer : _____

⑲  a.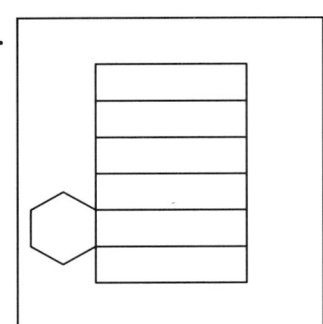

b. What is the solid that can be made from this net?

Answer : _____

c. How many rectangular faces does this solid have?

Answer : _____

⑳  a.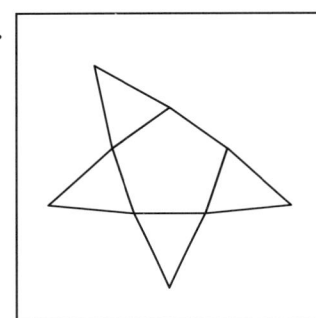

b. What is the solid that can be made from this net?

Answer : _____

c. How many triangular faces does this solid have?

Answer : _____

㉑  a.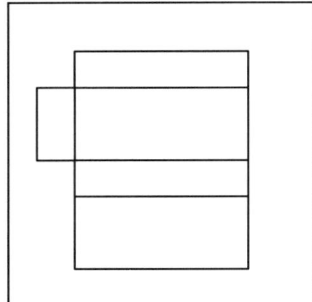

b. What is the solid that can be made from this net?

Answer : _____

c. How many rectangular faces does this solid have?

Answer : _____

㉒  a.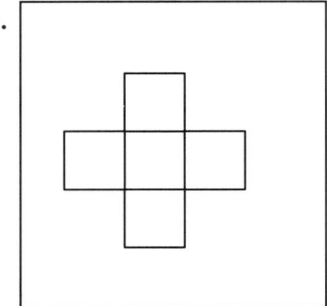

b. What is the solid that can be made from this net?

Answer : _____

c. Draw this solid on the dot paper.

## Look at the shapes. Solve the problems. Show your work.

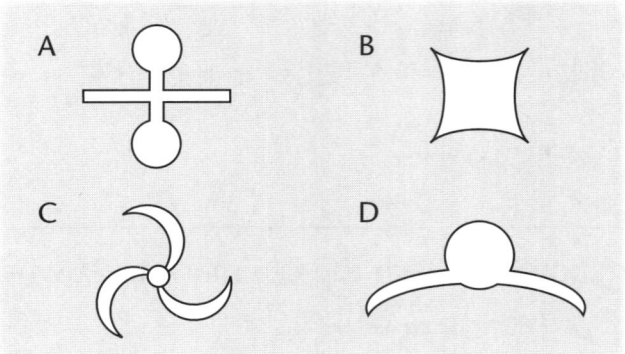

A pattern has rotational symmetry if it can be rotated about a point or a line. e.g.

**Read this first.**

This shape fits on itself 4 times in one complete rotation. It has rotational symmetry of order 4.

㉓ How many lines of symmetry does A have? Does it have rotational symmetry? If so, what is its order?

_Answer :_ _____

㉔ How many lines of symmetry does B have? Does it have rotational symmetry? If so, what is its order?

_Answer :_ _____

㉕ How many lines of symmetry does C have? Does it have rotational symmetry? If so, what is its order?

_Answer :_ _____

㉖ How many lines of symmetry does D have? Does it have rotational symmetry? If so, what is its order?

_Answer :_ _____

## CHALLENGE

Sally used 7 interlocking cubes to build a solid and she drew the top view of the solid. Help her draw the front and side view of the solid on the dot paper.

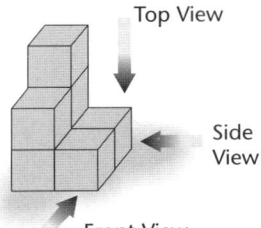

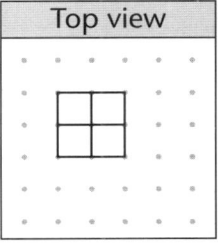

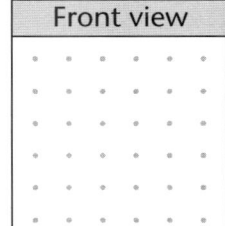

Kelly and Louis went to their favourite flea market which was 56.07 km from their house.

① What was the distance between the flea market and Kelly's house in metres?

*Answer :* _____

② They left home at 9:47 a.m. and took 42 minutes to reach the flea market. At what time did they arrive there?

*Answer :* _____

③ What was their average speed in kilometres per hour?

*Answer :* _____

④ If they wanted to reach the flea market 4 minutes earlier, at what speed would they have to drive then? (correct to the nearest whole number)

*Answer :* _____

⑤ Kelly was looking for a frame for her picture. Her picture was 48 cm long and 36 cm wide. What was the length and width of her picture in dm?

*Answer :* _____

⑥ What was the area of her picture in square centimetres?

*Answer :* _____

⑦ What was the perimeter of her picture?

*Answer :* _____

⑧ If Kelly wanted to leave a border of 2.5 cm on all sides of her picture, what would the the length and width of the frame be?

*Answer :* _____

⑨ What would the outside perimeter of the border be?

*Answer :* _____

⑩ The pattern on Kelly's frame is shown on the right. Does this pattern have lines of symmetry? If so, how many lines of symmetry does it have? Does it have rotational symmetry? If so, what is its order?

*Answer :* _____

⑪ The cost of the frame was $57.64. If Kelly bought the frame and gave the cashier two $50 bills, how could the cashier give her the change with the fewest bills or coins?

*Answer :* _____

⑫ Louis was looking for a paperweight. A booth displayed their paperweights as a tower. Draw the top, front, and side view of the tower in the space below to show how it looks.

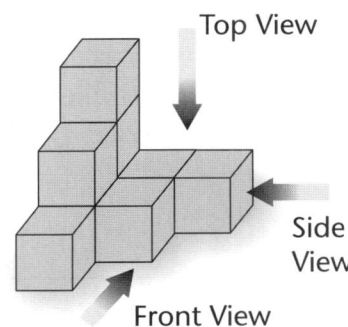

Top View

Side View

Front View

| Top View | Front View | Side View |
|---|---|---|
| | | |

⑬ If each side of a paperweight was 4 cm long, what was its volume?

*Answer :* _____

⑭ Louis bought 2 paperweights for $4.79 each. The cashier charged him an additional $1.29 for taxes. If the cashier gave him the change with the fewest coins or bills, what was his change from a $20 bill?

*Answer :* _____

Sally has drawn 2 nets on a piece of cardboard.

A.

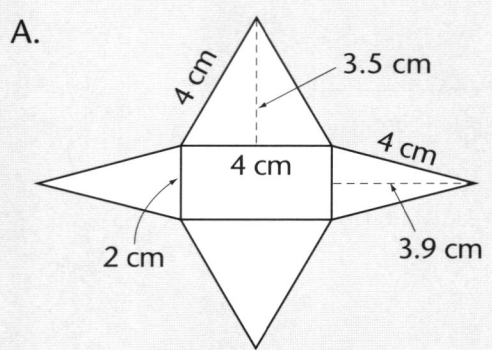

B.

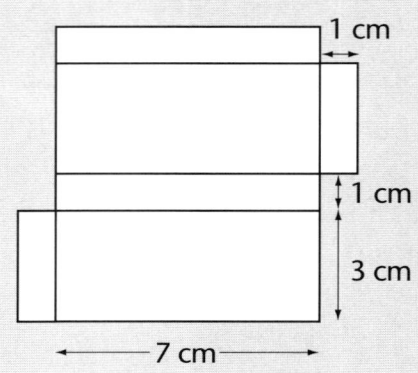

⑮ What is the solid which can be made from net A?

Answer : _____

⑯ What is the solid which can be made from net B?

Answer : _____

⑰ How many square centimetres of cardboard does Sally need to make net A?

Answer : _____

⑱ How many square centimetres of cardboard does Sally need to make net B?

Answer : _____

⑲ If Sally cuts out net A and makes solid A, how many edges does solid A have?

Answer : _____

⑳ If Sally decorates solid A by putting a braid along each edge, how long will the braid be?

Answer : _____

㉑ If the cost of the braid is $0.16 per cm, how much will Sally pay for the braid?

Answer : _____

㉒ Sally cuts out net B and makes solid B. What is the volume of solid B?

Answer : _____

㉓ Draw solid B on the dot paper.

## Circle the correct answer in each problem.

㉔ How many centimetres are there in one kilometre?

    A.  1 000 cm        B.  1 000 000 cm   C.  10 000 cm      D.  100 000 cm

㉕ If Emily buys 160 g of candies every day for a week, how many kilograms of candies will she have at the end of the week?

    A.  1.02 kg        B.  11.2 kg        C.  1.12 kg       D.  1120 kg

㉖ If a car travels at an average speed of 45.8 km/h, how far will it go between 9:45 a.m. and 2:30 p.m.?

    A.  194.65 km    B.  217.55 km    C.  240.45 km    D.  222.13 km

㉗ Peter wants to paint an area in the shape of a parallelogram 1.45 m long and 0.84 m high.  What is the area of the parallelogram in square centimetres?

    A.  121.8 cm²    B.  12 180 cm²   C.  121 800 cm²   D.  12 280 cm²

㉘ If Joan changes her $5 bill into quarters, how many quarters will she get?

    A.  20          B.  12          C.  200         D.  40

㉙ Rebecca says, 'I have five thousand six hundred four dollars and three cents'.  How much does Rebecca have?

    A.  $5640.03     B.  $5604.30     C.  $5604.03     D.  $5640.30

㉚ A rectangular box is 1.4 m long, 0.5 m wide and 0.8 m high.  What is its volume?

    A.  0.56 m³      B.  5.6 m³       C.  4.6 m³       D.  0.46 m³

㉛ How many litres of water can the rectangular box hold?

    A.  5600 L      B.  5.6 L        C.  56 L        D.  560 L

㉜ The area of a triangle is 7.15 cm².  If the base is 2.2 cm, what is its height?

    A.  1.625 cm    B.  3.25 cm    C.  7.865 cm    D.  6.5 cm

## EXAMPLE

Graph each set of ordered pairs and join them in order. What shape is it?

A(0, 4), B(7, 4), C(9, 0), D(2, 0)

Think : (0, 4)

move 4 units up
from (0, 0)

move 0 unit right from (0, 0)

*Answer :* It is a parallelogram.

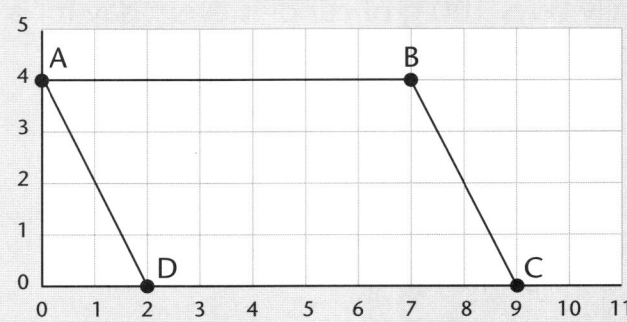

## Solve the problems. Show your work.

Fred and Ted were doodling on some graph paper. Help them graph each set of ordered pairs and join them to form polygons. Then identify each polygon.

① (0, 5), (7, 3), (7, 0), (0, 0)

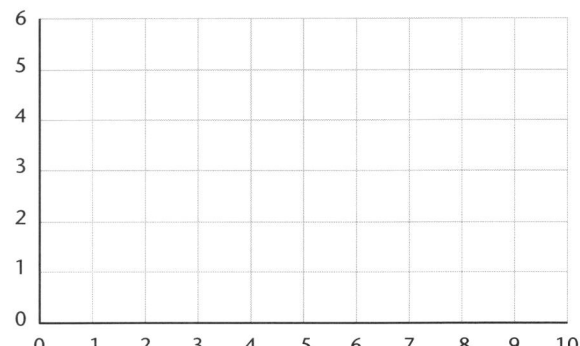

*Answer :* It is a _____ .

② (3, 0), (1, 3), (3, 6), (6, 6), (8, 3), (6, 0)

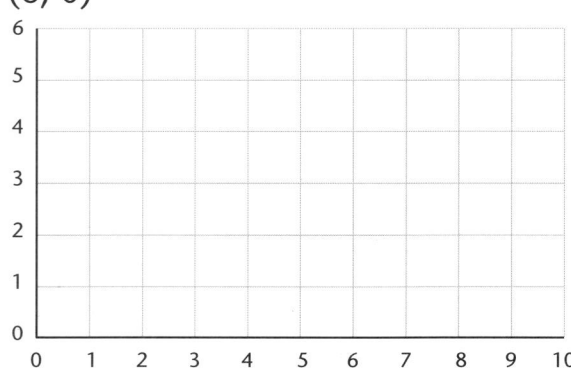

*Answer :* _____

③ (2, 0), (0, 2), (0, 4), (2, 6), (4, 6), (6, 4), (6, 2), (4, 0)

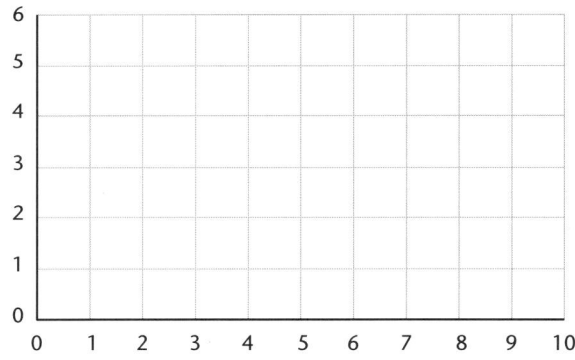

*Answer :* _____

④ (3, 0), (1, 3), (5, 6), (9, 3), (7, 0)

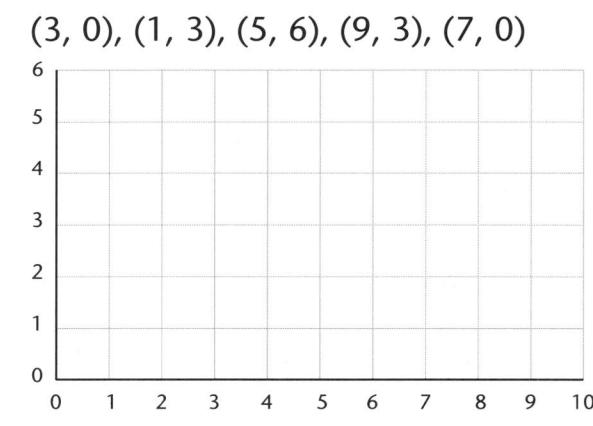

*Answer :* _____

Mr Lister draws a grid over the map of St. Louis Zoo. Use his grid to find the coordinates of all the places and locate the public washrooms.

⑤ The gate is at ( ___ , ___ ).

⑥ The Patting Zoo is at ( ___ , ___ ).

⑦ The Butterfly House is at ( ___ , ___ ).

⑧ The Insect Dome is at ( ___ , ___ ).

⑨ The Restaurant is at ( ___ , ___ ).

⑩ The Gift Shop is at ( ___ , ___ ).

⑪ The Stage is at ( ___ , ___ ).

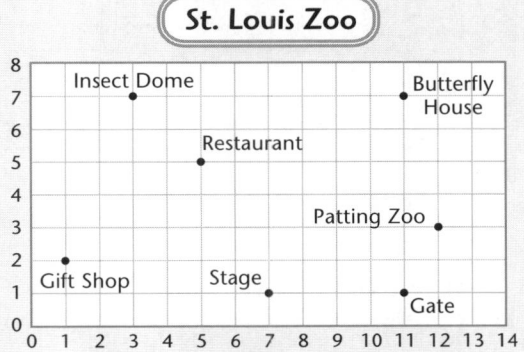

⑫ There are 5 public washrooms. They are at (10, 1), (8, 7), (4, 6), (3, 4) and origin. Label them A, B, C, D and E respectively.

⑬ Mr Lister sets a route for his class. Follow his instructions and join the places in order to show the route.

| Entrance gate | → | Stage | → | Patting Zoo | → | Butterfly House | → | Insect Dome | → | Restaurant | → | Gift Shop |

⑭ Larry wants to enlarge the map with a scale two times larger than the original. Help him label the axes and all the places in the zoo on the grid below. Then join the places to show the route.

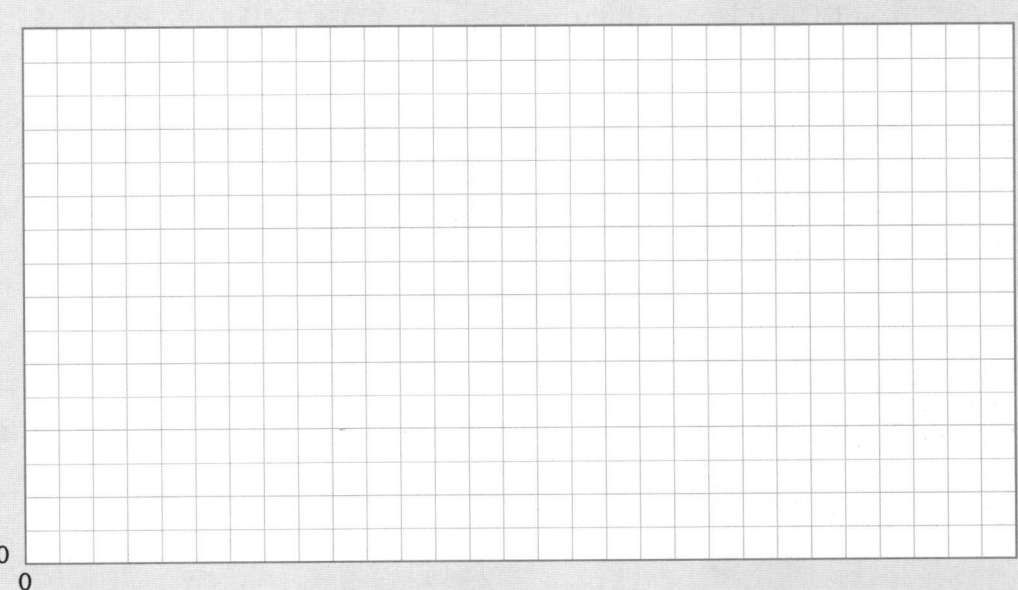

Miss Led decided to set up her classroom on a grid.  Write the names of the children in the boxes and solve the problems.

⑮

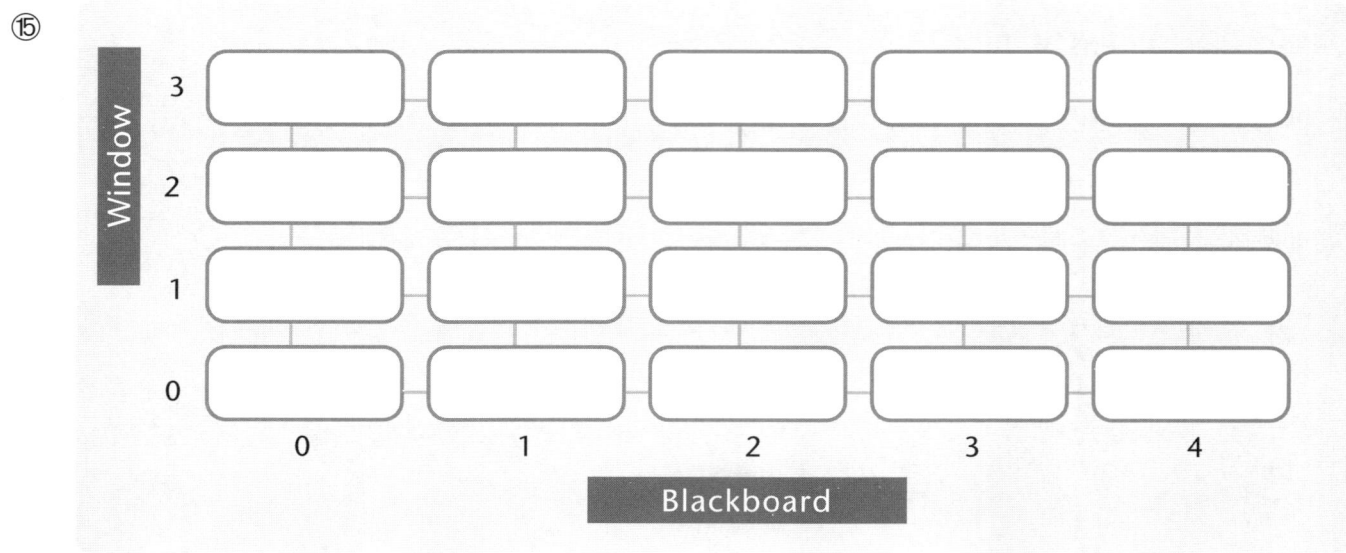

⑯   Uma was assigned (1, 0) and her best friend, Emily, was assigned (4, 3).  Would they be happy with the seating?  Explain.

*Answer :* _____

⑰   The three most talkative students, Ted, George and Jiffy, were assigned (4, 2), (3, 2) and (3, 1) respectively.  Would this be a good idea if the teacher wanted a quiet class?  Explain.

*Answer :* _____

⑱   Billy always complained about reflection from the sun in his glasses.  If you were Miss Led, would you assign Billy to sit at (0, 1) or (3, 3)?  Explain.

*Answer :* _____

⑲   Rebecca had trouble hearing the teacher.  If you were Miss Led, would you assign Rebecca to sit at (2, 0) or (1, 3)?  Explain.

*Answer :* _____

⑳   Miss Led said that she didn't want Olive, Gerry or Terry to sit beside each other.  If Olive was assigned (1, 2), which seats couldn't the other 2 sit at?

*Answer :* _____

㉑ Gerry was the tallest student in the class. Miss Led wanted to assign Gerry and Terry to sit at (0, 0) or (0, 3). Where should each sit? Explain.

*Answer :* _____

㉒ Miss Led wanted to assign Raymond and Louis to sit beside Olive, but she knew that Raymond was George's best friend. Where should Raymond and Louis sit? Explain.

*Answer :* _____

㉓ Elaine's seat was between Raymond and Terry. Stephanie's seat was between Louis and Rebecca. Write the ordered pairs of Elaine's and Stephanie's seats.

*Answer :* _____

㉔ Katherine sat in front of Olive and David sat behind Olive. Write the ordered pairs of Katherine's and David's seats.

*Answer :* _____

㉕ Vera's seat was 2 units right and 1 unit down from Katherine's seat. Write the ordered pairs of Vera's seat.

*Answer :* _____

㉖ How many empty seats were there in the class? Write the ordered pairs of the empty seats.

*Answer :* _____

# CHALLENGE

Larry went skiing. He used the following points to show his run. Could he easily ski this run?

(0, 7), (2, 6), (4, 5), (5, 4), (7, 4), (8, 3), (11, 5), (12, 1), (13, 0)

*Answer :* _____

 **Transformations**

## EXAMPLE

Ivy moves a triangle 3 units left and 2 units down and labels the translated image I. She then flips figure I over the line *l* and labels the flipped image II. What will be the ordered pairs of the vertices of figure II?

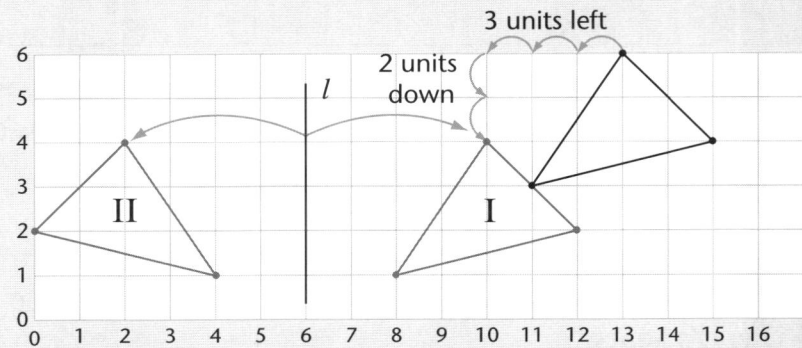

*Answer :* The vertices of figure II are (2, 4), (0, 2) and (4, 1).

## Solve the problems. Show your work.

① Which figures are the translation images of the shaded triangle?

*Answer :* _____ are the translation images of the shaded triangle.

② Which figures are the rotation images of the shaded figure?

*Answer :* _____

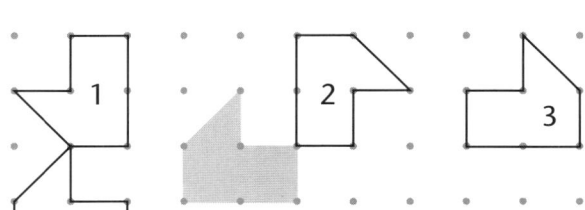

③ Which figures are the reflection images of the shaded figure?

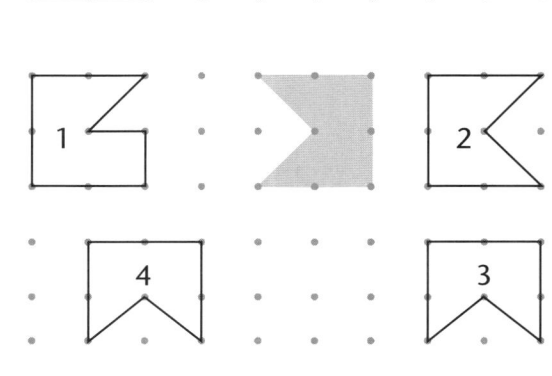

*Answer :* _____

## Draw the figures on the grids and solve the problems.

④ a. Translate the figure 3 units left and 3 units down. Then label it I.

b. Turn figure I 180° about the point (5, 3). Then label it II.

c. What are the ordered pairs of the vertices of figure II?

*Answer :* The ordered pairs of the vertices are _____ .

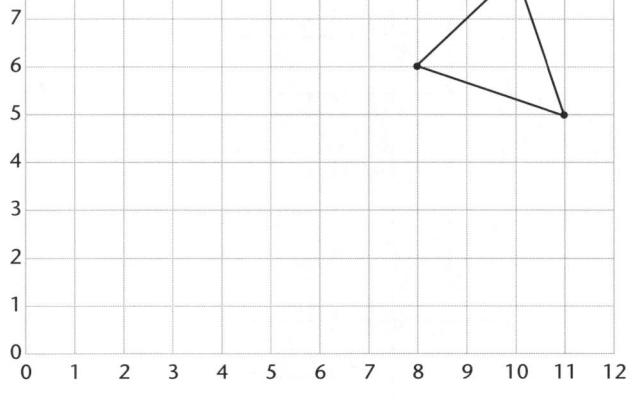

⑤ a. Flip the figure over the line *l*. Then label it I.

b. Translate figure I 5 units right and 3 units up. Then label it II.

c. What are the ordered pairs of the vertices of figure II?

*Answer :* _____

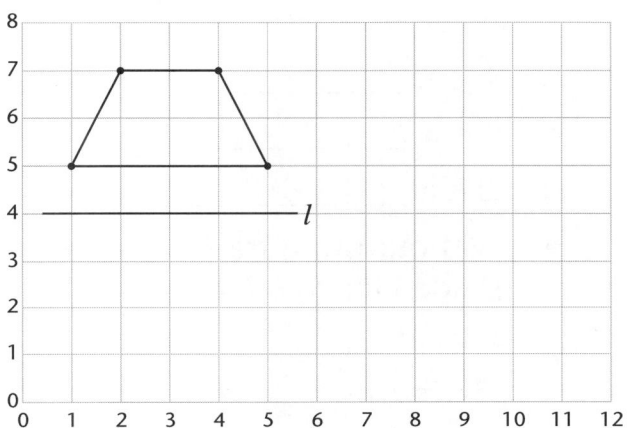

⑥ a. Turn the figure $\frac{1}{4}$ counterclockwise about the point (7, 5). Then label it I.

b. Flip figure I over the line *l*. Then label it II.

c. What are the ordered pairs of the vertices of figure II?

*Answer :* _____

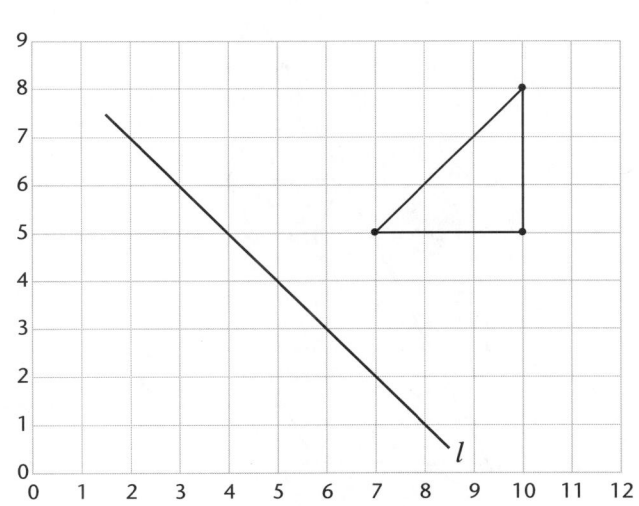

⑦ After translation, rotation or reflection of a figure, is the image congruent with, or similar to, the original figure?

*Answer :* _____

## Complete the tiling patterns and solve the problems.

⑧    a.

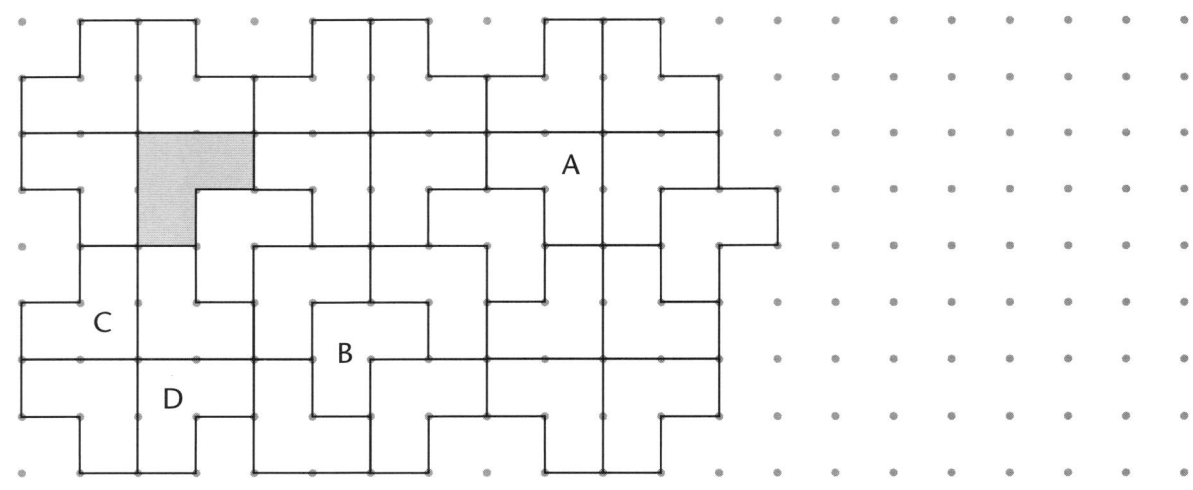

b.    A is a _____ image of the shaded tile.

c.    B is a _____ image of the shaded tile.

d.    C is a _____ image of the shaded tile.

e.    Without using translation, what transformation(s) will you use to transfer the shaded tile to D?  How?

      *Answer :* _____

⑨    a.

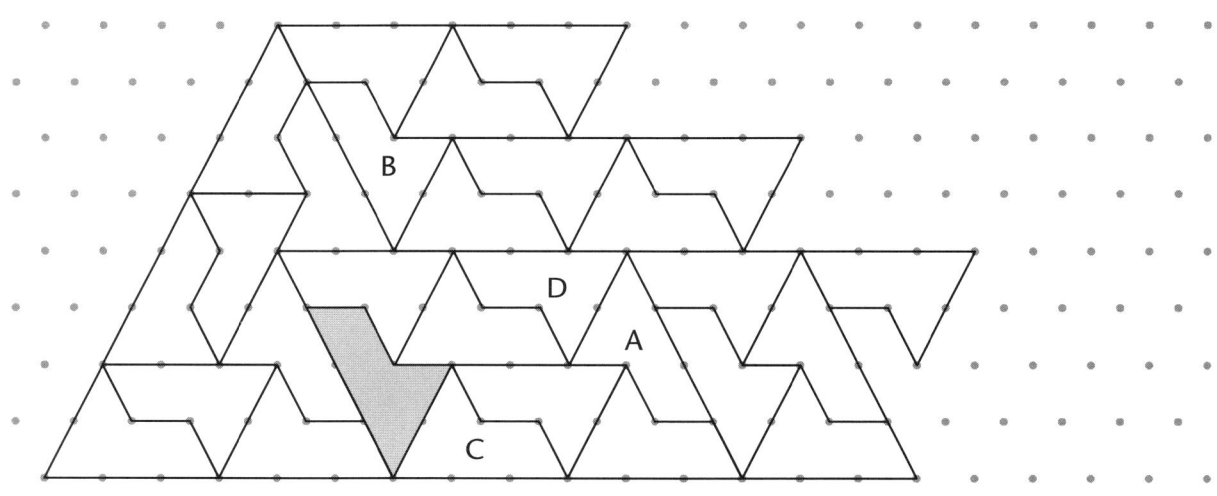

b.    A is a _____ image of the shaded tile.

c.    B is a _____ image of the shaded tile.

d.    C is a _____ image of the shaded tile.

e.    What transformation(s) will you use to transfer the shaded tile to D?

      *Answer :* _____

Joan has to find one of the keys below to open the treasure chest. If she picks the wrong one, she will be trapped. Follow the clues to draw lines on the grid to find the reflection image of the figure on the right key.

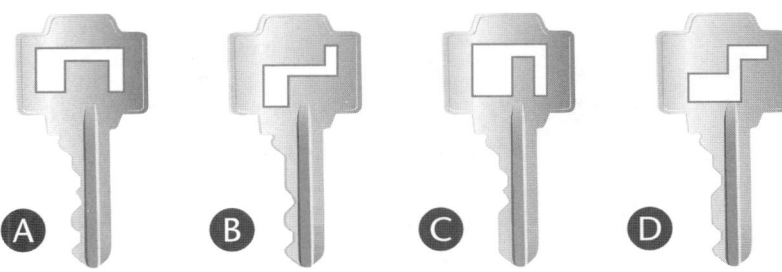

Mark all the points as you go.

⑩

- Begin at start and go upward 3 units.

- Turn $\frac{1}{4}$ counterclockwise and go forward 4 units.

- Turn $\frac{1}{4}$ clockwise and go forward 3 units.

- Turn $\frac{1}{4}$ counterclockwise and go forward 2 units.

- Turn $\frac{1}{4}$ counterclockwise and go forward 4 units.

- Turn $\frac{1}{4}$ counterclockwise and go forward 5 units.

Start

- Turn $\frac{1}{4}$ clockwise and go forward 2 units.

- Turn $\frac{1}{4}$ counterclockwise and go forward 1 unit.

⑪ Which is the key to open the treasure chest?

Answer : _____

# CHALLENGE

Jimmy used 2 transformations to transfer each shaded figure to the labelled figure. Describe each translation, rotation and reflection clearly.

①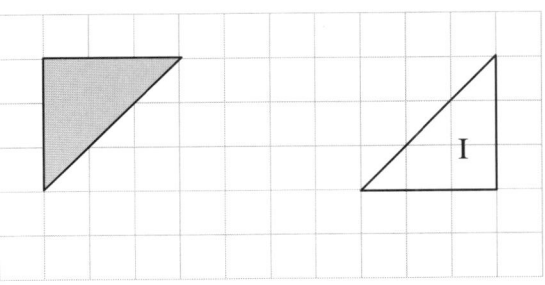

②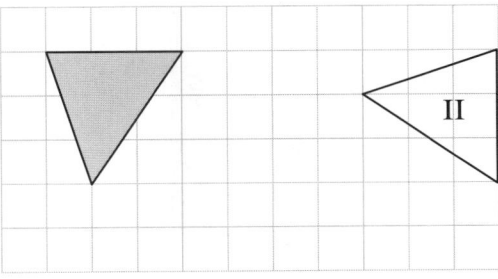

Answer : _____       Answer : _____

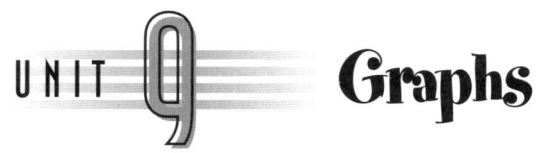

# UNIT 9 Graphs

## EXAMPLE

Look at Peter's table which shows his earnings in the past 6 months.  Use his table to make a bar graph and a line graph.

| Month | Jan | Feb | Mar | Apr | May | Jun |
|-------|-----|-----|-----|-----|-----|-----|
| Earnings ($) | 200 | 300 | 300 | 500 | 800 | 600 |

a.  Bar graph

b.  Line graph

## Solve the problems.  Show your work.

Barney kept track of the number of books borrowed each week in his school library.

| Week | 1st | 2nd | 3rd | 4th | 5th | 6th |
|------|-----|-----|-----|-----|-----|-----|
| No. of fiction books borrowed | 70 | 75 | 65 | 50 | 40 | 70 |
| No. of non-fiction books borrowed | 55 | 90 | 60 | 50 | 15 | 45 |

① Use his table to complete the bar graph.

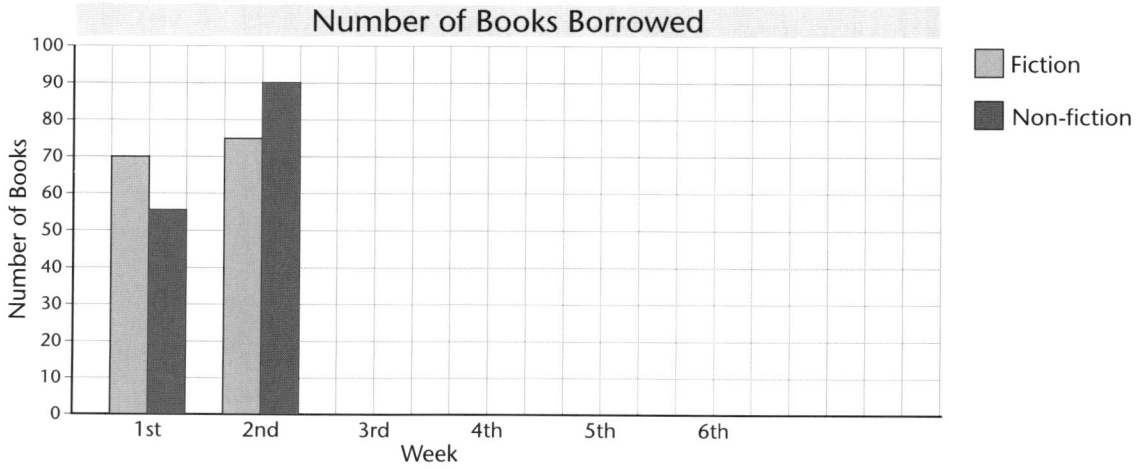

② How many more fiction books were borrowed than non-fiction books in the 1st week?

*Answer :*

③ In which week was the number of fiction books borrowed the same as the number of non-fiction books borrowed?

*Answer :*

④ In which week was the number of non-fiction books borrowed more than the number of fiction books borrowed?

*Answer :*

⑤ How many fiction books were borrowed over the six weeks?

*Answer :*

⑥ How many non-fiction books were borrowed over the six weeks?

*Answer :*

⑦ There were only 3 school days in one of the past 6 weeks. Which week was it? Explain.

*Answer :*

⑧ When Barney checked over the Math books, he found that a quarter of them were textbooks, a quarter activity books and the rest workbooks.

Types of Math Books

a. Draw a circle graph to show the types of Math books.

b. If there were 120 Math books, how many were activity books?

*Answer :*

c. How many were workbooks?

*Answer :*

Brenda and Tammy used a table to record their spending on groceries each month.

| | Brenda's spending | Tammy's spending |
|---|---|---|
| JAN | $275 | $325 |
| FEB | $300 | $200 |
| MAR | $250 | $75 |
| APR | $350 | $200 |
| MAY | $175 | $225 |
| JUN | $225 | $300 |

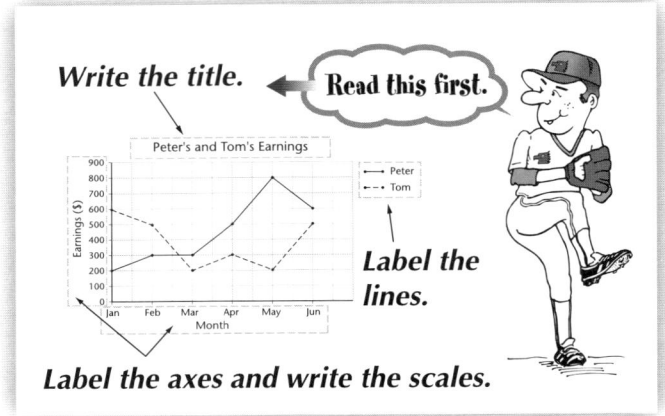

⑨ Use a line graph to show their spending.

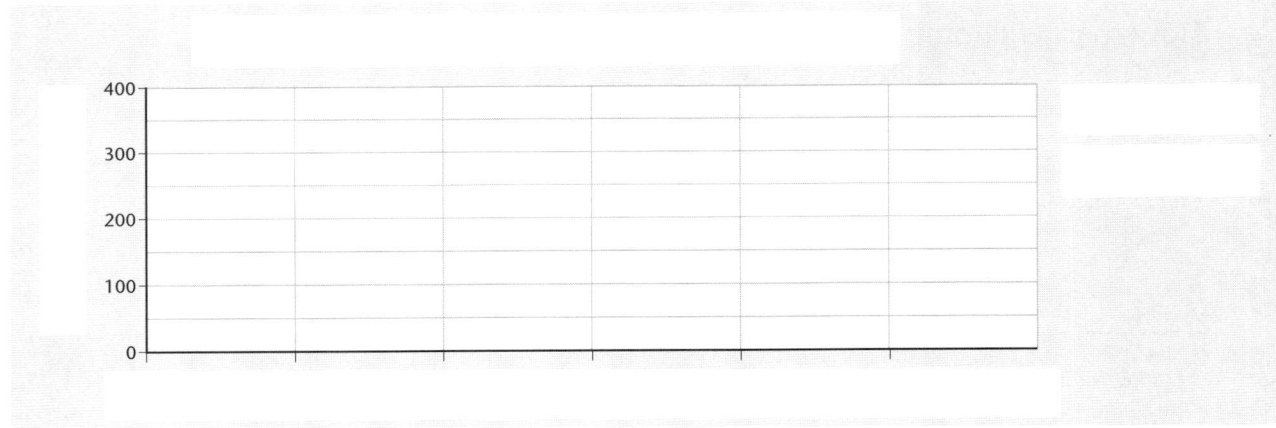

⑩ How much more did Brenda spend than Tammy in April?

Answer : _____

⑪ How much more did Tammy spend than Brenda in June?

Answer : _____

⑫ In which month did Brenda spend the most on groceries?  How much more when compared with the month she spent the least?

Answer : _____

⑬ In which month did Tammy spend the least on groceries?  How much less when compared with the month she spent the most?

Answer : _____

⑭ In which month was the difference between Brenda's and Tammy's spending the greatest?

Answer : _____

⑮ Who spent more money in the six months? How much more?

Answer : _____

⑯ In February, one-third of Brenda's spending was on meat, one-sixth on vegetables and the rest on fruit. Use a circle graph to show Brenda's spending in February.

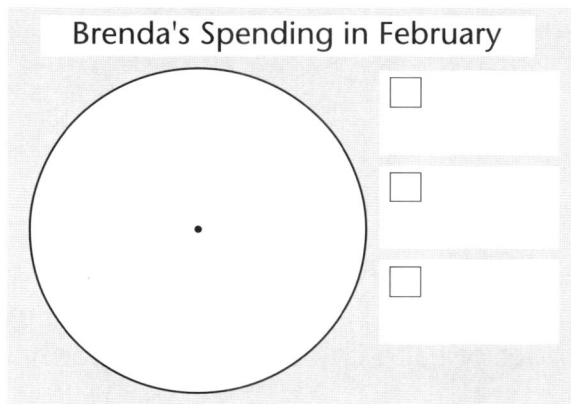

Brenda's Spending in February

⑰ How much did Brenda spend on meat in February?

Answer : _____

⑱ How much did Brenda spend on fruit in February?

Answer : _____

⑲ In February, a quarter of Tammy's spending was on meat, one-eighth on vegetables and the rest on fruit. Use a circle graph to show Tammy's spending in February.

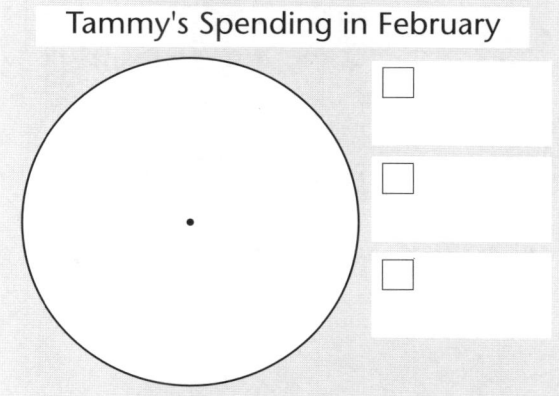

Tammy's Spending in February

⑳ How much did Tammy spend on fruit in February?

Answer : _____

㉑ Did Tammy spend more money on fruit than Brenda in February? Explain.

Answer : _____

# CHALLENGE

① Measure the angle of each sector to complete the table.

| Marble | Red | Yellow | Blue | Green |
|--------|-----|--------|------|-------|
| Angle  |     |        |      |       |

② If Tim had 120 red marbles, how many green marbles did he have?

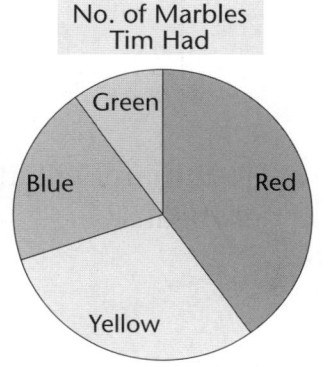

No. of Marbles Tim Had

Answer : _____

## EXAMPLE

Louie kept track of the number of apples he ate each month on a circle graph. Which month did Louie eat the most apples? If Louie ate 5 apples in December, would you assume that Louie liked apples? Explain.

Think : Louie ate the most apples in November since that is the largest area in the circle graph. If Louie ate 5 apples in December, it would mean he ate just a few more than 5 in November and fewer than 5 in January. Louie probably didn't like apples that much.

**Monthly Apple Consumption**

November

December    January

*Answer :* Louie ate the most apples in November and he probably didn't like apples.

## Use the graphs to solve the problems. Show your work.

Each month, Jody's grandfather brought her a bag of jellybeans. Jody liked jellybeans, especially the red ones. She noticed that the number of red jellybeans varied from month to month and decided to keep track of the number of each colour on a line graph.

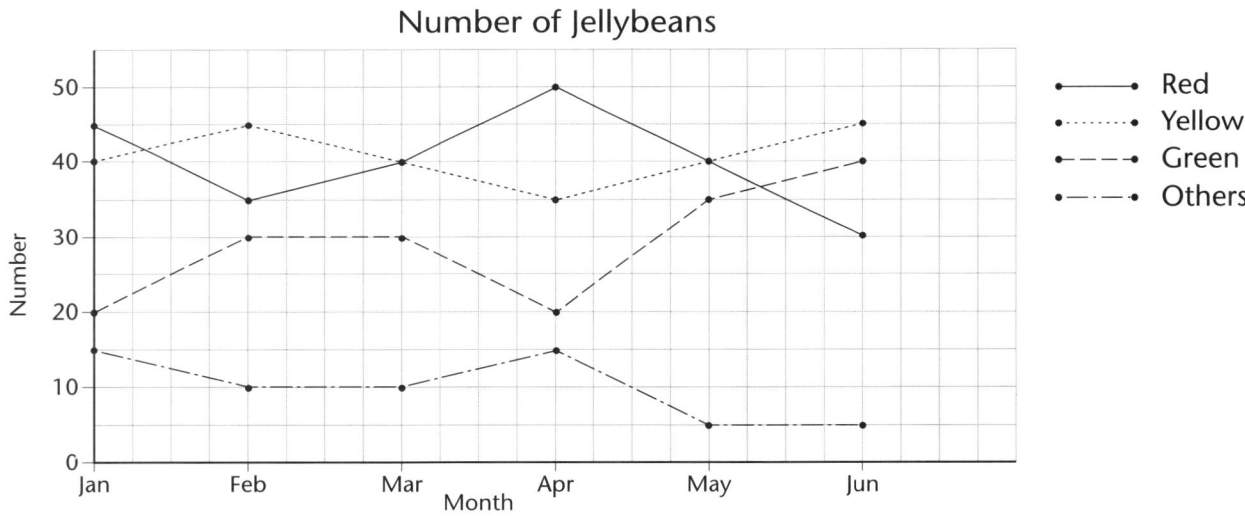

Number of Jellybeans

① How many jellybeans were in a bag? Did each bag have the same number of jellybeans?

*Answer :* _____ jellybeans were in a bag. Each bag _____ .

② In which month would Jody be happiest with her jellybeans? Explain.

Answer : _____

③ In which month would Jody be unhappiest with her jellybeans? Explain.

Answer : _____

④ In which month did Jody get the least yellow jellybeans?

Answer : _____

⑤ How many more green jellybeans than red jellybeans did Jody get in June?

Answer : _____

⑥ If the company making the jellybeans discovered that the red jellybeans were the most expensive to make, can you tell when they made this discovery?

Answer : _____

⑦ Describe the change in the number of yellow jellybeans between April and June.

Answer : _____

⑧ If this tendency had continued, how many yellow jellybeans do you think Jody would have got in July?

Answer : _____

⑨ Describe the change in the number of red jellybeans between April and June.

Answer : _____

⑩ If this tendency had continued, how many red jellybeans do you think Jody would have got in July?

Answer : _____

⑪ What was the median number of red jellybeans Jody got for the past 6 months?

Answer : _____

*The median in a set of numbers is the middle number when the numbers are arranged in order. If there are 2 middle numbers, take their average as the median.*

Read this first.

e.g.  1  3  ⑨  12  15
*9 is the median.*

1  3  ⟨7  9⟩  12  15

*median : (7 + 9) ÷ 2 = 8*

*8 is the median.*

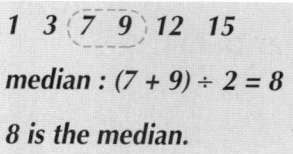

Every student in Fred's class had to record the number of vehicles passing a certain point. Fred kept track of the vehicles near a construction site for 2 hours.

⑫    Use Fred's graph to complete the table.

| Vehicle | Tally | Frequency |
|---------|-------|-----------|
| Car |  |  |
| Van |  |  |
| Jeep |  |  |
| Truck |  |  |
| Bus |  |  |

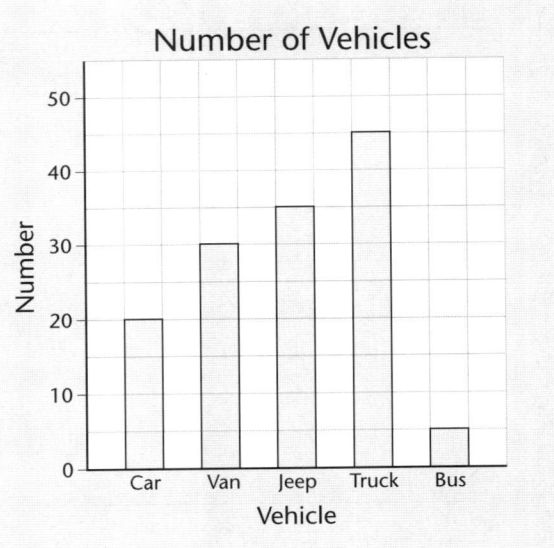

⑬    How many cars did Fred see?

Answer : _____

⑭    How many more Jeeps than vans did Fred see?

Answer : _____

⑮    How many vehicles did Fred see in all?

Answer : _____

⑯    On average, how many vehicles did Fred see per hour?

Answer : _____

⑰    If Fred did the recording near his home, do you think that he would collect similar data?

Answer : _____

⑱    Fred's friend, Peter, did his survey and made a bar graph shown below.

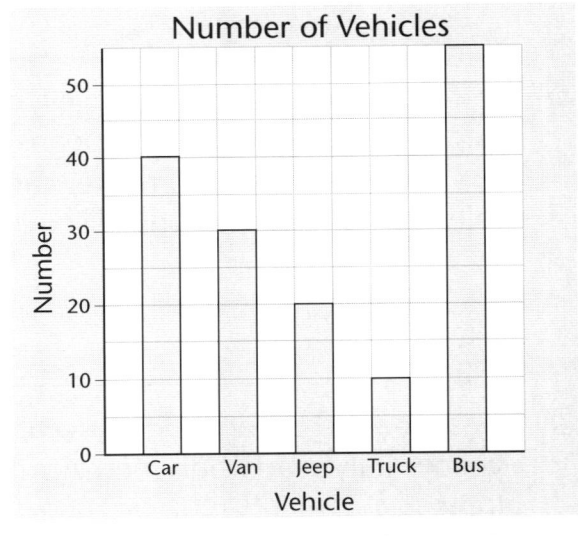

a.    Can you tell where Peter collected the data?

Answer : _____

b.    In what ways are Fred's graph and Peter's graph the same?

Answer : _____

Peter and Darlene kept track of the postal deliveries to their house each month on a bar graph.

⑲ What type of mail did they receive the most each month?

Answer : _____

Postal Deliveries

⑳ Why do you think they received more magazines in January than November or December?

Answer : _____

㉑ In which month did they receive the most letters?

Answer : _____

㉒ Why do you think they received the most letters in that month?

Answer : _____

㉓ In which month did they receive the most junk mail?

Answer : _____

㉔ Why do you think they received the most junk mail in that month?

Answer : _____

# CHALLENGE

Mrs Diaz measures the heights of 5 of her students. Their heights are 165 cm, 137 cm, 140 cm, 151 cm and 144 cm. If Peter joins the 5 students, the median height will be 143 cm.

① How tall is Peter?

② What is the mean height?

Answer : _____

Answer : _____

## EXAMPLE

Paula has a bag with 1 red marble, 1 yellow marble and 1 green marble. She picks 1 marble from the bag and flips a coin. How many possible outcomes are there? What is the probability that she will get a green marble and a head?

Think :  There are 3 marbles and 1 coin. Use a tree diagram to find all the possibilities.

Write :  Tree diagram

| Marble | Coin | Result |
|--------|------|--------|
| Red | H | (R, H) |
|  | T | (R, T) |
| Yellow | H | (Y, H) |
|  | T | (Y, T) |
| Green | H | (G, H) |
|  | T | (G, T) |

Possible outcomes :

(R, H), (R, T), (Y, H), (Y, T), (G, H), (G, T)

There are 1 out of 6 chances to get a green marble and flip a head.

P(green ball and head) $= \dfrac{1}{6}$

Answer :  There are 6 possible outcomes. The probability that Paula will get a green marble and a head is $\dfrac{1}{6}$.

## Solve the problems.  Show your work.

Charlie has a bag. It contains 10 marbles, 2 red, 2 yellow, 2 green, 2 blue and 2 white. All the marbles have the same size and weight. Marley is going to draw a marble from Charlie's bag.

① How many possible outcomes are there?

Answer :  There are _____ .

② What is the probability that the marble will be blue?

Answer : _____

③ What is the probability that the marble will be green or yellow?

Answer : _____

| R | Red |
|---|-----|
| B | Blue |
| G | Green |
| Y | Yellow |
| W | White |

④ Is each outcome equally likely? Explain.

Answer : _____

⑤ Marley has drawn a green marble from the bag. If he is to draw one more from the remaining marbles, will the outcomes be equally likely? Explain.

*Answer :* _____

⑥ Charlie puts 3 more white marbles and 2 more yellow marbles in his bag and then asks Marley to draw a marble again. How many possible outcomes are there? What are they?

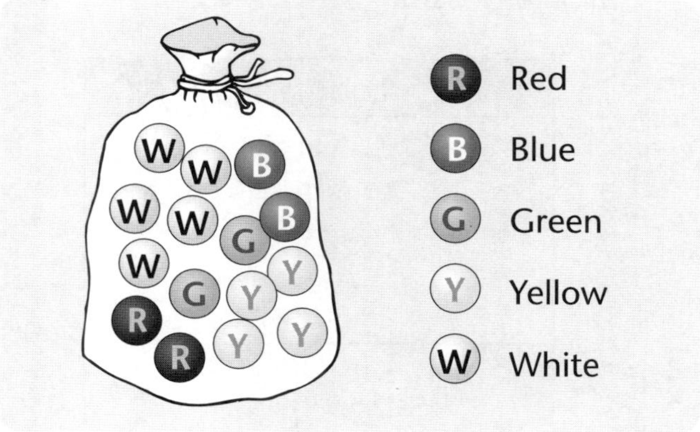

| R | Red |
| B | Blue |
| G | Green |
| Y | Yellow |
| W | White |

*Answer :* _____

⑦ Are the outcomes equally likely? Explain.

*Answer :* _____

⑧ What is the most likely outcome if a marble is drawn?

*Answer :* _____

⑨ What is the probability that the marble will be red?

*Answer :* _____

⑩ What is the probability that the marble will be white?

*Answer :* _____

⑪ Charlie says, 'If I draw out a marble from my bag now, the most likely marble is yellow'. Is he correct? Explain.

*Answer :* _____

⑫ If Charlie wants each outcome to be equally likely, at least how many more marbles does he need to put into the bag? What are they?

*Answer :* _____

Sally makes 5 cards marked 1, 2, 3, 4 and 5 and turns them face down on a table. She shuffles the cards and lines them up. Gary has a loonie. They try to select 1 card and flip the coin once. After every pick, the card is put back and is shuffled with other cards.

⑬ Complete the tree diagram to show all the possible outcomes.

| Card | Loonie | Result |
|------|--------|--------|
| 1 | H | ( 1, H ) |
|   | T | ( 1, T ) |
|   |   |   |
|   |   |   |
|   |   |   |
|   |   |   |

⑭ How many possible outcomes are there?

Answer : _____

⑮ Are the outcomes equally likely?

Answer : _____

⑯ What is the probability that they will get a 1 and a head?

Answer : _____

⑰ What is the probability that they will get a 5 and a tail?

Answer : _____

⑱ What is the probability that they will get an even number and a head?

Answer : _____

⑲ What is the probability that they will get an odd number and a tail?

Answer : _____

⑳ The player who gets a 1 and a head first win. Sally goes first and gets a 2 and a head. What is the probability that Gary will win?

Answer : _____

㉑ Gary says, 'If both Sally and I lost in our first try, Sally will have a greater chance to win than before'. Is he correct? Explain.

Answer : _____

Sally uses her 5 cards to play another game with Gary. This time, she shuffles the cards and lets Gary draw 2 cards.

㉒ Draw a tree diagram to show all the possible outcomes.

| 1st draw | 2nd draw | Result |
| --- | --- | --- |
|  |  |  |
|  |  |  |
|  |  |  |
|  |  |  |
|  |  |  |

After drawing out 1 card, there are 4 cards left.

$$\left(\begin{array}{l}\text{1st draw : 5 cards} \\ \text{2nd draw : 4 cards}\end{array}\right)$$

**Read this first.**

㉓ How many possible outcomes are there?

Answer : _____

㉔ Is each outcome equally likely?

Answer : _____

㉕ What is the probability that Gary will get 2 even numbers?

Answer : _____

㉖ What is the probability that he will get 2 cards that add up to 6 or more?

Answer : _____

㉗ What is the probability that he will get 2 cards that add up to 1?

Answer : _____

㉘ What is the probability that he will get 2 cards with the same number?

Answer : _____

# CHALLENGE

Joan spun one of the spinners on the right 60 times. The spinners landed on A 9 times, B 19 times and C 32 times. Which spinner did Joan likely spin? Explain.

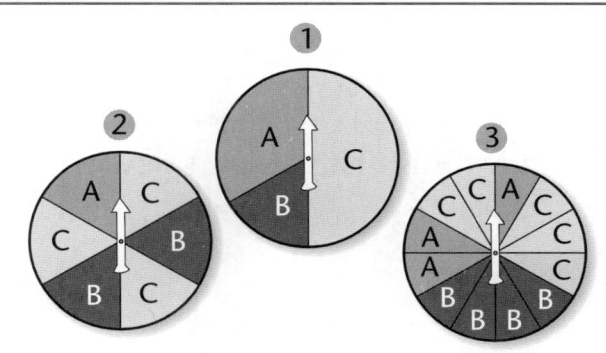

Answer : _____

**Solve the problems. Show your wrok.**

Mr Bush recorded the number of toothbrushes produced by his factory last year.

① How many toothbrushes were produced in the 1st quarter?

Answer : _____

② How many toothbrushes were produced in the 3rd quarter?

Answer : _____

③ How many more toothbrushes were produced in the 4th quarter than in the 2nd quarter?

Answer : _____

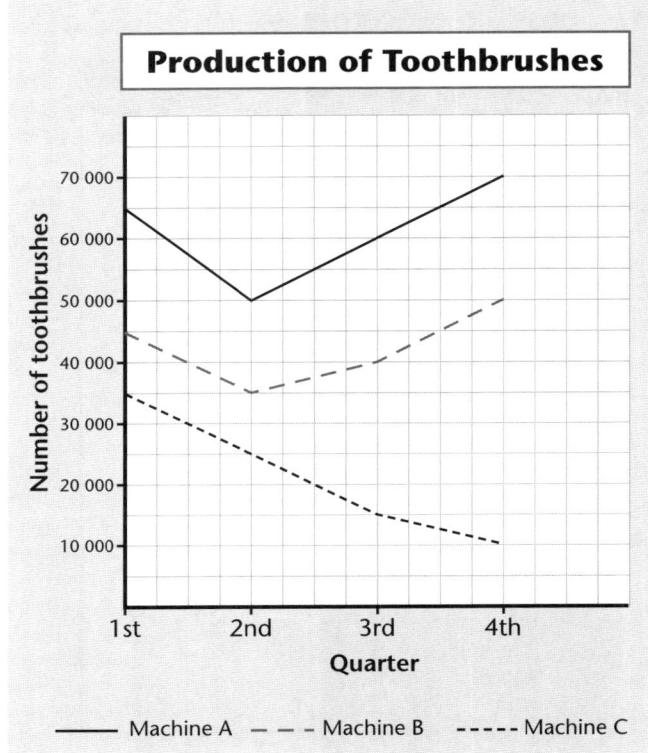

**Production of Toothbrushes**

—— Machine A  – – – Machine B  - - - - - Machine C

④ If each toothbrush cost $0.53, how much money would Mr Bush have collected last year?

Answer : _____

⑤ Describe the change in the number of toothbrushes produced by machine A.

Answer : _____

⑥ Describe the change in the number of toothbrushes produced by machine C.

Answer : _____

⑦ If Mr Bush had to shut down the least efficient machine, which one would it be? Explain.

Answer : _____

⑧ Use the clues to find the locations of the places. Mark the places on the grid and find the coordinates.

- Wellness Drug Mart is 4 units up from Bond's Convenience Store.

- Family Mart is 2 units left from Wellness Drug Mart.

- Echo Convenience Store is 4 units right and 3 units up from Bond's Convenience Store.

- Mayor Mart is 5 units right from Echo Convenience Store.

- Al's Bargain Place is 2 units left and 9 units up from Mayor Mart.

- Venus Mart is 1 unit right and 9 units up from the origin.

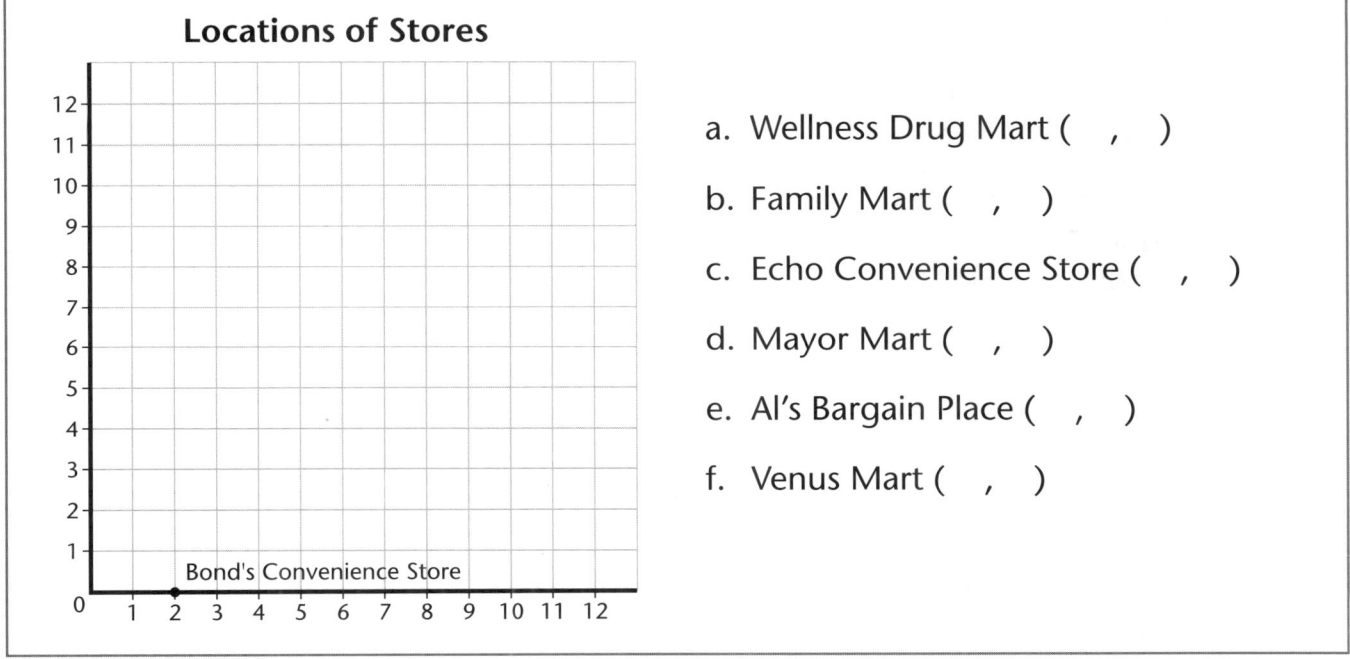

a. Wellness Drug Mart ( , )

b. Family Mart ( , )

c. Echo Convenience Store ( , )

d. Mayor Mart ( , )

e. Al's Bargain Place ( , )

f. Venus Mart ( , )

⑨ Mr Bush sets a delivery route. Follow his instructions and join the places in order to show the route on the grid.

Bond's Convenience Store → Echo Convenience Store → Mayor Mart → Al's Bargain Place → Venus Mart → Wellness Drug Mart → Family Mart

⑩ If the delivery man left Bond's Convenience Store at 1:46 p.m. and took 3 hours 35 minutes to complete the deliveries, at what time did he finish the job?

Answer : _____

⑪ The distance between Mayor Mart and Al's Bargain Place is 18.9 km. If the delivery man drove at an average speed of 60 km/h, how long would he take to drive from Mayor Mart to Al's Bargain Place?

Answer : _____

Carl lives in downtown near a public car park. He records the number of vehicles entering the parking lot from 9:00 a.m. to noon.

⑫    Use Carl's table to draw a bar graph.

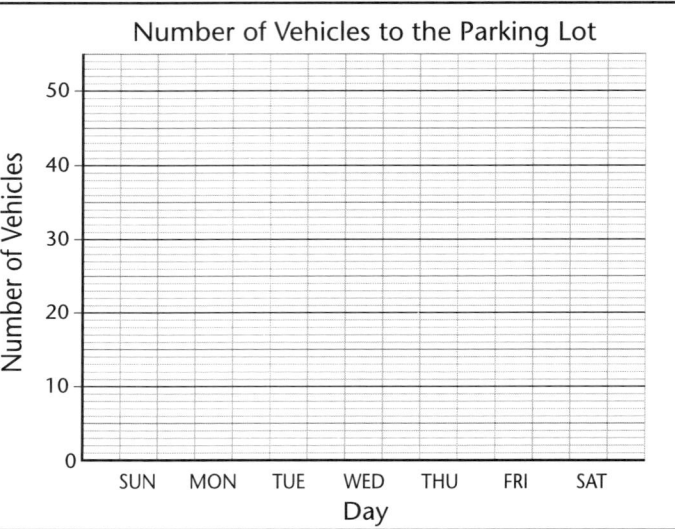

| Day | Number of Vehicles |
|-----|--------------------|
| SUN | 15 |
| MON | 25 |
| TUE | 33 |
| WED | 38 |
| THU | 42 |
| FRI | 43 |
| SAT | 12 |

⑬    How would you describe the bars on the graph to compare the volume of traffic throughout the week?

*Answer :* _____

⑭    Explain the sharp drop on Saturday and Sunday.

*Answer :* _____

⑮    What was the median number of vehicles entering the car park?

*Answer :* _____

⑯    Carl found that 14 vans, 21 cars and 7 Jeeps drove into the parking lot on Thursday. Draw a circle graph to show the types of vehicles. What fraction of the vehicles were vans?

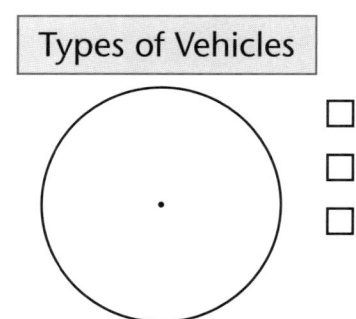

Types of Vehicles

*Answer :* _____

⑰    If one of the vehicles in question 16 left the parking lot, what would be the probability that it was a van?

*Answer :* _____

⑱ There were only 1 car, 1 Jeep and 1 van in the parking lot and a driver came to pick up his or her vehicle. Complete the tree diagram to show all the possible outcomes.

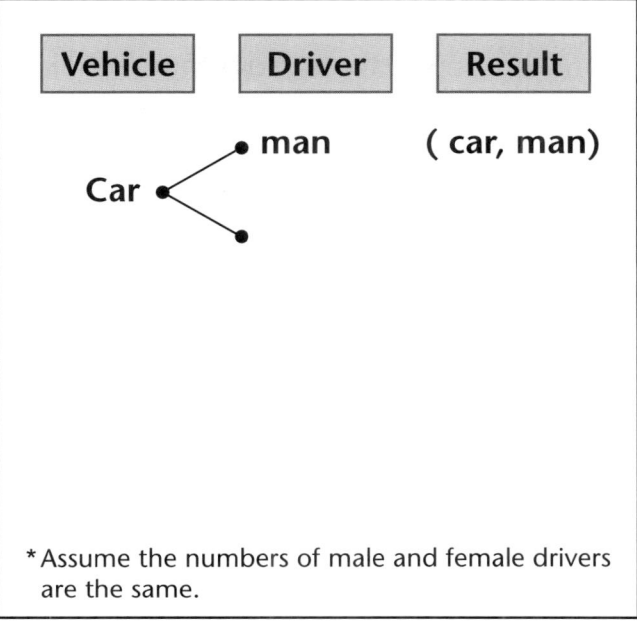

| Vehicle | Driver | Result |

man ( car, man)

Car

*Assume the numbers of male and female drivers are the same.

⑲ What would be the probability that a male driver came to pick up the Jeep?

Answer : _____

⑳ If there were 3 cars, 1 Jeep and 1 van in the parking lot, what would be the probability that a female driver came to pick up her car?

Answer : _____

㉑ The parking lot is rectangular in shape with an area of 612 m². The length of the parking lot is 25.5 m long. What is its width?

Answer : _____

㉒ The total area of the lanes is one-third of the whole parking lot. If the parking space for a vehicle is 3.4 m long and 2 m wide, how many parking spaces will there be?

Answer : _____

㉓ What is the perimeter of the parking lot?

Answer : _____

㉔ Look at the signs below.

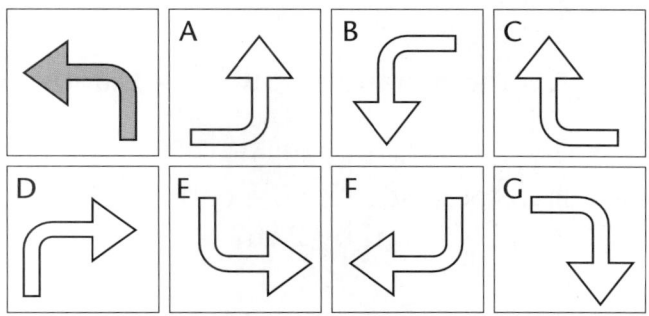

A   B   C

D   E   F   G

a. Which signs are the rotation images of the shaded sign?

Answer : _____

b. Which signs are the reflection images of the shaded sign?

Answer : _____

㉕ The parking fee for the 1st hour is $3.25 and $2.15 for every extra half hour. A whole day ticket is $18.00. If Mr Winter parked his car in the car park for 3 hours 48 minutes, would it be wise to buy a whole day ticket?

Answer : _____

# FINAL REVIEW

## Circle the correct answer in each problem.

㉖ How many millimetres are there in a metre?

    A. 10 mm     B. 100 mm     C. 1000 mm     D. 10 000 mm

㉗ If Jimmy spends $7.75 on magazines and $2.50 on newspapers, how much change will he get from a $20 bill?

    A. $10.25     B. $9.75     C. $9.65     D. $9.25

㉘ Which has the greatest area : a rectangle 5 cm by 8 cm, a triangle with base 18 cm and height 6 cm, a parallelogram with base 12 cm and height 3 cm, or a square with sides 7 cm?

    A. the rectangle     B. the triangle     C. the parallelogram     D. the square

㉙ If water cost $12.50 a cubic metre, how much would it cost to fill a rectangular tank 3 m by 2.5 m by 2 m?

    A. $187.50     B. $177.50     C. 188.50     D. 178.50

㉚ How many faces does a triangular pyramid have?

    A. 3     B. 6     C. 5     D. 4

㉛ What is the order of rotational symmetry of the figure on the right?

    A. 4     B. 5

    C. 6     D. 7

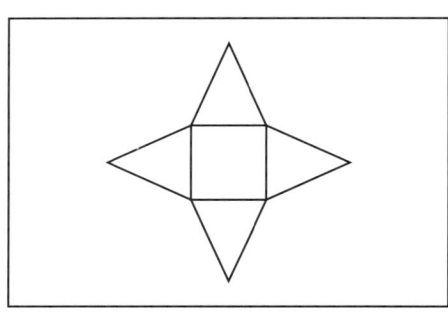

㉜ The figure in question 31 is a net of a geometric solid. If the net is folded, what geometric solid can you get?

    A. Triangular Prism     B. Rectangular Prism

    C. Square Pyramid     D. Triangular Pyramid

## Unit 1

1.

| m | 40 | 2 | 4500 | 800 | 950 | 700 |
|---|---|---|---|---|---|---|
| cm | 4000 | 200 | 450 000 | 80 000 | 95 000 | 70 000 |
| km | 0.04 | 0.002 | 4.5 | 0.8 | 0.95 | 0.7 |

2.

| g | 900 | 8300 | 50 | 290 | 60 000 | 3440 |
|---|---|---|---|---|---|---|
| kg | 0.9 | 8.3 | 0.05 | 0.29 | 60 | 3.44 |

3.

| mL | 2050 | 450 | 110 | 52 000 | 32 400 | 9 |
|---|---|---|---|---|---|---|
| L | 2.05 | 0.45 | 0.11 | 52 | 32.4 | 0.009 |

4. a. 40 cm + 8 dm = 40 cm + 80 cm = 120 cm      False
   b. 500 mm + 6 m = 50 cm + 600 cm = 650 cm      True
   c. 8.2 kg + 200 g = 8200 g + 200 g = 8400 g      True
   d. 0.5 L + 400 mL = 0.5 L + 0.4 L = 0.9 L      False
5. (1.3 kg = 1300 g)      Amount of candies : 1300 + 250 = 1550
   Kelly bought 1550 g of candies in all.
6. (0.75 kg = 750 g)      No. of times : 750 ÷ 100 = 7.5
   Milly would pay 7.5 times the price per 100 g.
7. (14 cm = 0.14 m, 1200 mm = 1.2 m)
   Amount of ribbon bought : 0.14 + 0.8 + 1.2 = 2.14
   They bought 2.14 m of ribbon.
8. 2.14 m = (2.14 x 100) cm = 214 cm      They bought 214 cm of ribbon.
9. (800 g = 0.8 kg)      Amount of candies : 1.03 + 0.8 = 1.83
   She bought 1.83 kg of candies.
10. (2.4 kg = 2400 g)      No. of bags : 2400 ÷ 600 = 4
    They bought 4 bags in all.
11. (2.25 L = 2250 mL)      Amount of juice : 2250 ÷ 5 = 450
    1 container held 450 mL of juice.
12. (450 mL = 0.45 L)      Difference : 0.89 – 0.45 = 0.44
    Container A could hold 0.44 L more juice than container B.

### Challenge

1. (6.4 m = 6400 mm)      No. of tiles : 6400 ÷ 8 = 800
   There were 800 tiles.
2. Weight : 18 x 800 = 14400   (14400 g = 14.4 kg)      It weighed 14.4 kg.

## Unit 2

1. Price (store B) : 41.52 – 5.25 = 36.27 (36.27 > 35.98)      A
2. Change : 50 – 35.98 = 14.02      Her change was $14.02.
   She was given 1 $10 bill, 2 twoonies and 2 pennies.
3. (0.7 kg = 700 g)      Cost : 1.49 x (700 ÷ 100) = 10.43
   It would cost her $10.43.
4. Change : 12 – 10.43 = 1.57      Her change was $1.57.
   She was given 1 loonie, 2 quarters, 1 nickel and 2 pennies.
5. Cost per gram (store C) : 3.95 ÷ 125 = 0.0316
   Cost per gram (store D) : 2.99 ÷ 100 = 0.0299 (0.0299 < 0.0316)
   Store D's shoe polish was a better buy.
6. No. of quarters : 10 ÷ 0.25 = 40      He would get 40 quarters.
7. Cost : 2.49 x 2 + 1.25 = 6.23
   He would pay 3 twoonies, 2 dimes and 3 pennies.
8. Amount of money : (2.49 + 1.39 + 1.25) x 8 = 41.04
   She had $41.04.
9. Amount of money : (11.16 ÷ 4) x 3 = 8.37      She got back $8.37.
10. Total cost of popcorn and drink : 4.32 x 3 = 12.96
    Total cost of popcorn : 4.59 x 2 = 9.18
    Cost : 12.96 – 9.18 = 3.78      The jumbo soft drink cost $3.78.
11. Money Jeffrey had : 0.25 x 4 + 0.1 x 24 + 0.05 x 16 = 4.2
    (4.2 > 3.78)
    Yes, Jeffrey had enough money to buy a jumbo soft drink.
12. Money earned : 7.05 x 18 = 126.9
    He could earn $126.90 per week.
13. Bus fare per week : 1.85 x 2 x 6 =22.2
    Money earned : 126.9 – 22.2 = 104.7
    He earned $104.70.

14. Money earned : 104.7 – 25.38 = 79.32
    He earned $79.32.
15. No. of weeks : 600 ÷ 79.32 = 7.56 (2 decimal places)
    He would have to work 8 weeks.
16. Parking fee : 1.75 + 3 x 4 = 13.75      It was $13.75.
17. Parking fee : 1.75 + 3 x 3 = 10.75
    Money Mr Keller gave : 10.75 + 1.25 = 12      Mr Keller gave $12.00.
18. No. of nickels : 5 ÷ 0.05 = 100      He would get 100 nickels.
19. five thousand nine hundred seventy-five dollars and forty-five cents
20. six thousand ninety-four dollars
21. four thousand two hundred ten dollars and thirty cents
22. three thousand nine hundred eighty-one dollars and ninety-five cents
23. five thousand seven hundred dollars and forty cents
24. nine thousand eight dollars and ten cents

### Challenge

25, 5, 10, 5, 5
Amount of money : 2 x 25 + 1 x 5 + 0.25 x 10 + 0.1 x 5 + 0.05 x 5
= 58.25      Gary had $58.25.
He had enough money to trade for a $50 bill.

## Unit 3

1. Time taken : (1040 ÷ 1000) ÷ 0.08 = 13      13 min
2. Time taken : 11 h – 10 h 42 min = 18 min      Speed : 2160 ÷ 18 = 120
   He should walk 120 m/min (0.12 km/min).
3. Time taken : (2160 ÷ 1000) ÷ 0.08 = 27
   Time arrived : 10 h 42 min + 27 min = 11 h 9 min
   He would reach Elaine's house at 11:09 a.m.
4. Average speed : 506 ÷ 9.2 = 55      Their average speed was 55 km/h.
5. Time taken : 9.2 – (2 + 45 ÷ 60) – (3 + 30 ÷ 60) = 2.95
   He drove 2.95 hours (2 h 57 min).
6. Distance : 72 x 6 + 50 x (1 + 33 ÷ 60) = 509.5
   They drove 509.5 km.
7. Average speed : 300 ÷ (3 + 12 ÷ 60) = 93.75
   Their average speed was 93.75 km/h.
8. Total time taken : 36 ÷ 60 + 36 ÷ 40 = 1.5 (1 h 30 min)
   Time returned : 12 h 44 min + 1 h 30 min = 14 h 14 min
   She returned at 2:14 p.m.
9. Time : 2 h 45 min + 2 h 18 min = 5 h 3 min
   They reached the museum at 5:03 p.m.
10. Average speed : 138.92 ÷ (2 + 18 ÷ 60) = 60.4
    Their average speed was 60.4 km/h.
11. Time : 5 h 3 min – 16 min = 4 h 47 min      It would be 4:47 p.m.
12. Time taken : 2 h 18 min – 16 min = 2 h 2 min (2.03 h)
    Speed : 138.92 ÷ 2.03 = 68.43
    They would have to drive at 68.43 km/h.

### Challenge

Time taken : 6 h 15 min – 2 h 45 min = 3 h 30 min
Distance travelled by car : 80 x (3 + 30 ÷ 60) = 280
Distance travelled by truck : 50 x (3 + 30 ÷ 60) = 175
Distance between the two places : 280 + 175 = 455
The distance between Townville and Littleton was 455 km.

## Unit 4

1. Length : 10 x 4 = 40      40 cm
2. Length : (16 + 18) x 2 = 68      The braid border would be 68 cm long.
3. Length : (10 + 12) x 2 = 44      The braid border would be 44 cm long.
4. Length : 17 x 2 + 12 = 46      The braid border would be 46 cm long.
5. Area : 10 x 10 = 100      The area was 100 cm$^2$.
6. Area : 16 x 18 = 288      The area was 288 cm$^2$.
7. Area : 12 x 9 = 108      The area was 108 cm$^2$.
8. Area : 12 x 16 ÷ 2 = 96      The area was 96 cm$^2$.
9. Area left : 100 – 6 x 6 = 64      There was 64 cm$^2$ of cardboard left.
10. Area left : 288 – 14 x 12 = 120
    There was 120 cm$^2$ of cardboard left.

11. a. Area left : 108 – 8 x 6 = 60    There was 60 cm$^2$ of cardboard left.
    b. Perimeter : (8 + 7) x 2 = 30    The perimeter was 30 cm.
12. Area left : 96 – 10 x 13 ÷ 2 = 31    There was 31 cm$^2$ of cardboard left.
13. Width : 180 ÷ 15 = 12    Its width was 12 m.
14. Wallpaper needed : 15 x 3 x 2 + 12 x 3 x 2 = 162
    162 m$^2$ of wallpaper would be needed.
15. Area : (15 – 2) x (12 – 2) = 130
    She would need 130 m$^2$ of carpeting.
16. Perimeter : 5 + 12 + 13 = 30    The perimeter was 30 m.
17. Area : 12 x 5 ÷ 2 = 30    She would need 30 m$^2$ of tiles.
18. No. of cans : (5 x 3 + 12 x 3 + 13 x 3) ÷ 5 = 18
    She would need 18 cans.
19. Area : 18 x 16 = 288    She would need 288 m$^2$ of carpeting.
20. 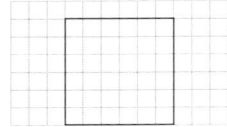    21.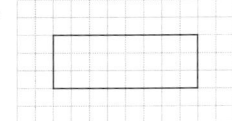

22. Suggested answer:    23. Suggested answer:

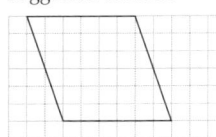    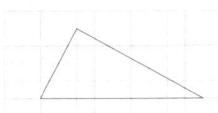

24. Suggested answer:    25. Suggested answer:

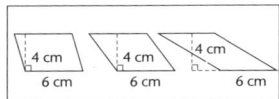    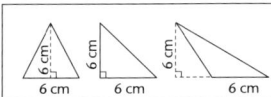

### Challenge

1. Perimeter : 10 + 30 + (24 – 8) + (18 – 6) = 68
   The perimeter is 68 cm.
2. Area : 18 x 24 – 24 x 18 ÷ 2 – 8 x 6 ÷ 2 = 192
   The area is 192 cm$^2$.

## Unit 5

1. 1 mL = 1 cm$^3$    Volume : 500 – 200 = 300    300 cm$^3$
2. Volume : 800 – 200 = 600    The volume is 600 cm$^3$.
3. Volume : 700 – 200 = 500    The volume is 500 cm$^3$.
4. Volume : 900 – 200 = 700    The volume is 700 cm$^3$.
5. D, B, C, A
6. Area : 300 ÷ 5 = 60    The area is 60 cm$^2$.
7. Length : 60 ÷ 6 = 10    Its length is 10 cm.
8. Area : 600 ÷ 6 = 100    The area is 100 cm$^2$.
9. Width : 100 ÷ 25 = 4    Its width is 4 cm.
10. Height : 700 ÷ 140 = 5    Its height is 5 cm.
11.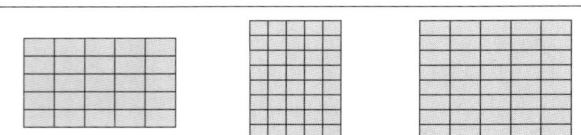

12. No. of layers : 40 ÷ 5 = 8    No. of bricks : (30 ÷ 6) x (50 ÷ 10) = 25
    There are 8 layers of 25 bricks each.
13. No. of bricks : 25 x 8 = 200
    200 bricks can be put in the container.
14. Amount of water : (50 x 30 x 40) ÷ 1000 = 60
    It can hold 60 L of water.
15. Width : 120 ÷ 15 = 8    Its width is 8 cm.
16. Height : 1500 ÷ 120 = 12.5    Its height is 12.5 cm.
17. Amount of water : 1500 cm$^3$ = 1500 mL = 1.5 L
    It can hold 1.5 L of water.
18. Volume : 0.5 x 0.45 x 0.2 = 0.045 (0.045 m$^3$ = 45000 cm$^3$)
    The volume is 0.045 m$^3$ (45 000 cm$^3$).

19. No. of pailfuls : 45000 ÷ 1500 = 30    She needs 30 boxes.
20. Volume : 1500 x 40 = 60000    The volume is 60 000 cm$^3$.
21. Area : 60000 ÷ 60 = 1000    Its base area is 1000 cm$^2$.
22. Height : 45000 ÷ 1000 = 45    It will be 45 cm high.
23. Volume : 30 x 21 x 1.8 = 1134    Its volume is 1134 m$^3$.
24. Amount of water : 1134 x 1000 = 1134000
    It can hold 1 134 000 L of water.
25. Volume : (30 x 21 x 1.6) x 1000 = 1008000
    There will be 1 008 000 L of water.
26. Amount of water : 30 x 21 x (1.7 – 1.6) x 1000 = 63000
    63 000 L of water should be pumped into the pool.
27. Time needed : 1134000 ÷ 30000 = 37.8    It will take 37.8 hours.
28. Height : (126000 ÷ 1000) ÷ (30 x 21) = 0.2    It will rise 0.2 m.

### Challenge

Volume : 4 x 9 x (5 + 4) + 4 x 4 x (16 – 9) = 436
Its volume is 436 cm$^3$.

## Unit 6

1. 4 cm, 4 cm, 4 cm; 60˚, 60˚, 60˚
2. 4 cm, 5 cm, 3 cm; 90˚, 37˚, 53˚
3. 4 cm, 4 cm, 4 cm; 60˚, 60˚, 60˚
4. 3 cm, 3.7 cm, 5.5 cm; 40˚, 110˚, 30˚
5. Triangles ABC and GHI are congruent because their corresponding sides and angles are equal.
6. Triangles ABC and GHI are acute triangles.
7. Triangle DEF is a right triangle.
8. Triangle JKL is an obtuse triangle.
9. Triangles ABC and GHI are equilateral triangles.
10. Triangles DEF and JKL are scalene triangles.
11. Suggested answer:

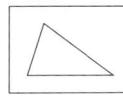

12. Triangular prism; 6, 5, 9    13. Rectangular pyramid; 5, 5, 8
14. Hexagonal prism; 12, 8, 18    15. Pentagonal pyramid; 6, 6, 10
16.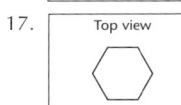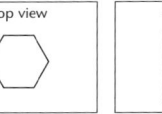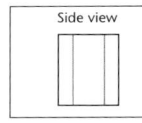

17.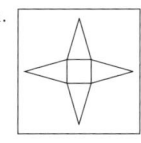

18. a. 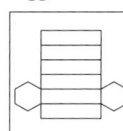    b. A square pyramid can be made from this net.
    c. It has 4 triangular faces.

19. a. Suggested answer: 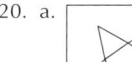    b. A hexagonal prism can be made from this net.
    c. It has 6 rectangular faces.

20. a. 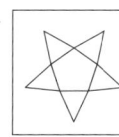    b. A pentagonal pyramid can be made from this net.
    c. It has 5 triangular faces.

21. a. Suggested answer:
    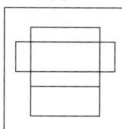
    b. A rectangular prism can be made from this net.
    c. It has 6 rectangular faces.

22. a. Suggested answer:
    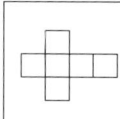
    b. A cube can be made from this net.
    c. Suggested answer:
    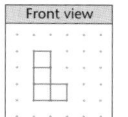

23. A has 2 lines of symmetry. It has rotational symmetry of order 2.
24. B has 4 lines of symmetry. It has rotational symmetry of order 4.
25. C has no line of symmetry. It has rotational symmetry of order 3.
26. D has 1 line of symmetry. It has no rotational symmetry.

**Challenge**

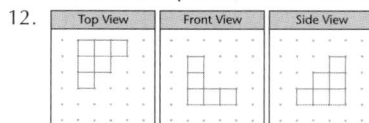

**Midway Review**

1. 56.07 km = (56.07 x 1000) m = 56070 m    The distance between the flea market and Kelly's house was 56 070 m.
2. Time : 9 h 47 min + 42 min = 10 h 29 min
   They arrived there at 10:29 a.m.
3. Speed : 56.07 ÷ (42 ÷ 60) = 80.1
   Their average speed was 80.1 km/h.
4. Speed : 56.07 ÷ ((42 − 4) ÷ 60) = 89
   They would have to drive 89 km/h.
5. Length : 48 ÷ 10 = 4.8   Width : 36 ÷ 10 = 3.6    The length and width of her picture were 4.8 dm and 3.6 dm respectively.
6. Area : 48 x 36 = 1728    The area of her picture was 1728 cm$^2$.
7. Perimeter : (48 + 36) x 2 = 168
   The perimeter of her picture was 168 cm.
8. Length : 48 + 2.5 x 2 = 53    Width : 36 + 2.5 x 2 = 41    The length and width of the frame would be 53 cm and 41 cm respectively.
9. Perimeter : (53 + 41) x 2 = 188
   The outside perimeter of the border would be 188 cm.
10. Yes, it has 4 lines of symmetry.
    It has rotational symmetry of order 4.
11. Change : 50 x 2 − 57.64 = 42.36
    The cashier could give her $42.36 change. There were 2 $20 bills, 1 twoonie, 1 quarter, 1 dime and 1 penny.
12.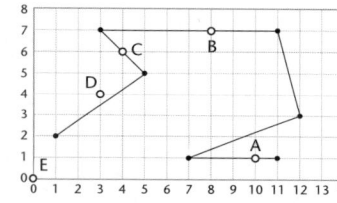
13. Volume : 4 x 4 x 4 = 64    Its volume was 64 cm$^3$.
14. Change : 20 − (4.79 x 2 + 1.29) = 9.13
    His change was $9.13. There were 1 $5 bill, 2 twoonies, 1 dime and 3 pennies.
15. It is a rectangular pyramid.
16. It is a rectangular prism.
17. Area : 4 x 2 + (4 x 3.5 ÷ 2) x 2 + (2 x 3.9 ÷ 2) x 2 = 29.8
    Sally needs 29.8 cm$^2$ of cardboard.
18. Area : 1 x 3 x 2 + 1 x 7 x 2 + 3 x 7 x 2 = 62
    Sally needs 62 cm$^2$ of cardboard.
19. Solid A has 8 edges.
20. Perimeter : 4 x 6 + 2 x 2 = 28    The braid will be 28 cm long.
21. Cost : 0.16 x 28 = 4.48    Sally will pay $4.48 for the braid.

22. Volume : 7 x 3 x 1 = 21    The volume is 21 cm$^3$.
23. Suggested answer:
    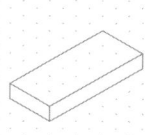

24. D    25. C    26. B    27. B    28. A
29. C    30. A    31. D    32. D

**Unit 7**

1.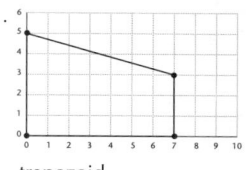
   trapezoid

2.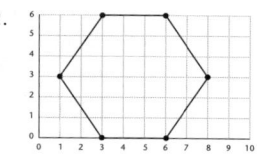
   It is a hexagon.

3.
   It is an octagon.

4.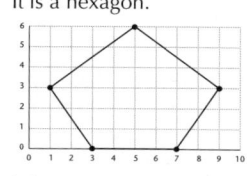
   It is a pentagon.

5. (11, 1)
6. (12, 3)
7. (11, 7)
8. (3, 7)
9. (5, 5)
10. (1, 2)
11. (7, 1)

12-13.
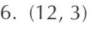

14.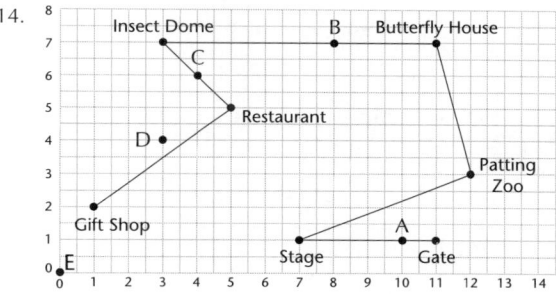

15.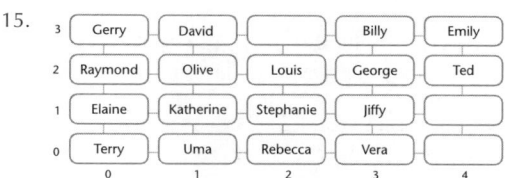

16. No, they are too far away from each other.
17. No, they are too close and will talk most of the time.
18. I would assign Billy to (3, 3) because the seat (0, 1) was close to the window.
19. I would assign Rebecca to (2, 0) so that she would be near the teacher.
20. They couldn't sit at (0, 2) or (2, 2).
21. Gerry should sit at (0, 3) and Terry at (0, 0), as Gerry should sit at the back.
22. Raymond should sit at (0, 2) and Louis at (2, 2) so that Raymond could not chat with George.
23. Elaine's seat was at (0, 1) and Stephanie's at (2, 1).
24. Katherine's seat was at (1, 1) and David's at (1, 3).

25. Vera's seat was at (3, 0).
26. There were 3 empty seats. They were at (2, 3), (4, 0) and (4, 1).

**Challenge**

No, Larry could not easily ski this run.

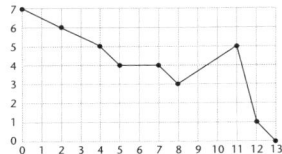

## Unit 8

1. 1 and 3
2. 1 and 2 are the rotation images of the shaded figure.
3. 2 and 3 are the reflection images of the shaded figure.
4. (2, 4), (3, 1) and (5, 3)

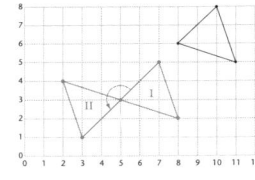

5. The ordered pairs of the vertices are (6, 6), (7, 4), (9, 4) and (10, 6).

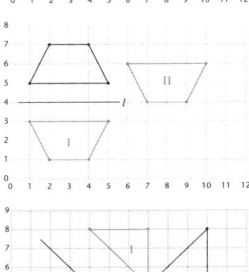

6. The ordered pairs of the vertices are (1, 5), (1, 2) and (4, 2).

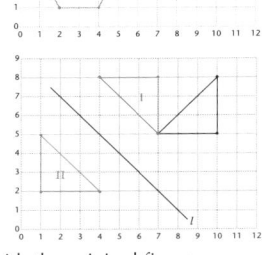

7. The image is congruent with the original figure.
8. a.

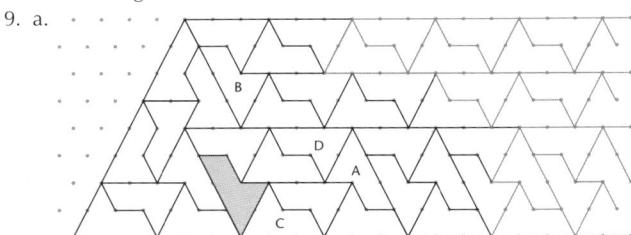

   b. reflection or rotation    c. translation    d. rotation
   e. Suggested answer: I will use 2 rotations to transfer the shaded tile to D. Rotate the shaded tile to get tile C first, and then rotate tile C to get D.
9. a.

   b. rotation    c. translation    d. reflection
   e. Suggested answer: I will use a reflection and a rotation to transfer the shaded tile to D. Flip the shaded tile to get tile C first, and then rotate tile C to get D.

10.

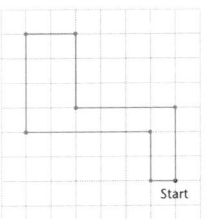

11. The key to open the treasure chest is B.

**Challenge**

1. Suggested answer:    2.

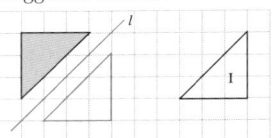 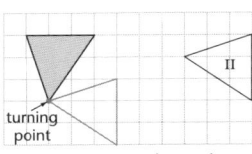

Use reflection and translation.

Flip the shaded figure over the line *l* and translate it 1 unit up and 6 units right.

Use rotation and translation.

Rotate $\frac{1}{4}$ clockwise about the turning point and translate it 2 units up and 6 units right.

## Unit 9

1.

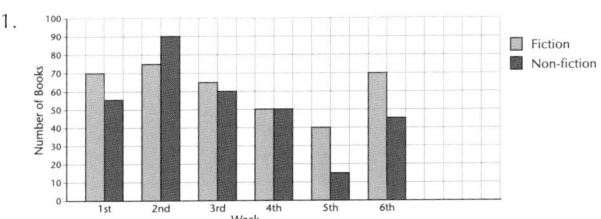

2. Difference : 70 − 55 = 15    15 more fiction books were borrowed.
3. It was the 4th week.
4. It was the 2nd week.
5. Total no. of books : 70 + 75 + 65 + 50 + 40 + 70 = 370
   370 fiction books were borrowed.
6. Total no. of books : 55 + 90 + 60 + 50 + 15 + 45 = 315
   315 non-fiction books were borrowed.
7. It was the 5th week because fewest number of books were borrowed.
8. a.

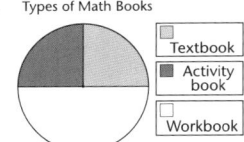

   b. No. of books : 120 ÷ 4 = 30    30 of them were activity books.
   c. No. of books : 120 ÷ 2 = 60    60 of them were workbooks.
9.

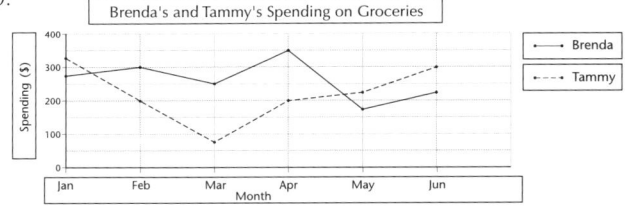

10. Difference : 350 − 200 = 150    Brenda spent $150 more.
11. Difference : 300 − 225 = 75    Tammy spent $75 more.
12. Difference : 350 − 175 = 175    It was April. It was $175 more.
13. Difference : 325 − 75 = 250    It was March. It was $250 less.
14. The greatest difference was in March.
15. Brenda's spending : 275 + 300 + 250 + 350 + 175 + 225 = 1575
    Tammy's spending : 325 + 200 + 75 + 200 + 225 + 300 = 1325
    Difference : 1575 − 1325 = 250
    Brenda spent $250 more than Tammy.

16. **Brenda's Spending in February**

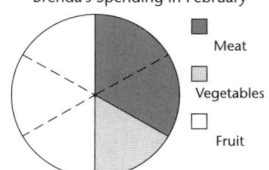

Legend:
- Meat (dark)
- Vegetables (light)
- Fruit (white)

17. Money spent : 300 ÷ 3 = 100
She spent $100 on meat.
18. Money spent : 300 ÷ 2 = 150
She spent $150 on fruit.

19. **Tammy's Spending in February**

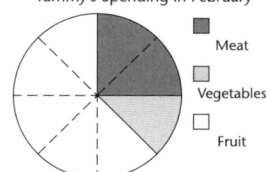

Legend:
- Meat (dark)
- Vegetables (light)
- Fruit (white)

20. Money spent : 200 ÷ 8 x 5 = 125
She spent $125 on fruit.
21. Brenda spent : $150
Tammy spent : $125
($150 > $125)  No, she didn't.

### Challenge

1. 144˚ , 108˚ , 72˚ , 36˚
2. The size of the angle of red marbles (144˚) is 4 times bigger than that of green marbles (36˚).
No. of green marbles : 120 ÷ 4 = 30  He had 30 green marbles.

## Unit 10

1.

| | Jan | Feb | Mar | Apr | May | Jun |
|---|---|---|---|---|---|---|
| No. of jellybeans | 120 | 120 | 120 | 120 | 120 | 120 |

120 ;  had the same no. of jellybeans

2. Jody would be happiest in April because she got the most red jellybeans.
3. She would be unhappiest in June because she got the least red jellybeans.
4. She got the least yellow jellybeans in April.
5. Difference : 40 – 30 = 10  She got 10 more.
6. They made the discovery in April when the number of red jellybeans started to decrease.
7. It is increasing by 5 every month.
8. No. of yellow jellybeans : 45 + 5 = 50
She would have got 50 yellow jellybeans in July.
9. It is decreasing by 10 every month.
10. No. of red jellybeans : 30 – 10 = 20
She would have got 20 red jellybeans in July.
11. No. of red jellybeans : 30, 35, ④⓪, ④⓪, 45, 50
Median : (40 + 40) ÷ 2 = 40  The median number was 40.

12.

| Vehicle | Tally | Frequency |
|---|---|---|
| Car | ∦∦ ∦∦ ∦∦ ∦∦ | 20 |
| Van | ∦∦ ∦∦ ∦∦ ∦∦ ∦∦ ∦∦ | 30 |
| Jeep | ∦∦ ∦∦ ∦∦ ∦∦ ∦∦ ∦∦ ∦∦ | 35 |
| Truck | ∦∦ ∦∦ ∦∦ ∦∦ ∦∦ ∦∦ ∦∦ ∦∦ ∦∦ | 45 |
| Bus | ∦∦ | 5 |

13. He saw 20 cars.
14. Difference : 35 – 30 = 5
He saw 5 more Jeeps.
15. Total of vehicles :
20 + 30 + 35 + 45 + 5 = 135
He saw 135 vehicles in all.
16. Average : 135 ÷ 2 = 67.5
He saw 67.5 vehicles on average.
17. No, he would not have seen as many trucks.
18. Suggested answer:
a. He might have collected his data near a bus terminal.
b. Their graphs have the same title, scale and label.
19. They received junk mail the most.
20. Suggested answer: They might receive some gift subscriptions.
21. It was December.
22. Suggested answer: They got Christmas cards in December.
23. It was December.
24. Suggested answer: They got more flyers for the Christmas season.

### Challenge

1.

median (143)

Height : 137, 140, ◯, 144, 151, 165

Peter's height : 143 x 2 – 144 = 142  Peter is 142 cm tall.
2. Mean: (165 + 137 + 140 + 151 + 144 + 142) ÷ 6 = 146.5
The mean height is 146.5 cm.

## Unit 11

1. 5 possible outcomes
2. The probability is $\frac{1}{5}$ .
3. 4 out of 10 marbles are green or yellow.
P(green or yellow) = $\frac{4}{10}$ = $\frac{2}{5}$  The probability is $\frac{2}{5}$ .
4. Yes, since each colour has the same number of marbles.
5. No, the outcomes will not be equally likely because the probability of drawing a green marble is $\frac{1}{9}$, but the probability of drawing a red, blue, yellow or white marble is $\frac{2}{9}$ .
6. There are 5 possible outcomes : red, blue, green, yellow or white.
7. No, since there are now more white and yellow marbles.
8. It is most likely a white marble.
9. 2 out of 15 marbles are red.  P(red) = $\frac{2}{15}$
The probability is $\frac{2}{15}$ .
10. 5 out of 15 marbles are white.  P(white) = $\frac{5}{15}$ = $\frac{1}{3}$
The probability is $\frac{1}{3}$ .
11. No, the most likely marble should be white.
12. There are 5 white marbles and 4 yellow marbles.  To make each outcome equally likely, he needs to put in 10 more : 3 red, 3 blue, 3 green and 1 yellow.

13.

| 1 | H | ( 1, H ) |
|---|---|---|
|   | T | ( 1, T ) |
| 2 | H | ( 2, H ) |
|   | T | ( 2, T ) |
| 3 | H | ( 3, H ) |
|   | T | ( 3, T ) |
| 4 | H | ( 4, H ) |
|   | T | ( 4, T ) |
| 5 | H | ( 5, H ) |
|   | T | ( 5, T ) |

14. There are 10 possible outcomes.
15. Yes.
16. 1 out of 10 outcomes is a 1 and a head.
P(1 & H) = $\frac{1}{10}$  The probability is $\frac{1}{10}$ .
17. 1 out of 10 outcomes is a 5 and a tail.
P(5 & T) = $\frac{1}{10}$  The probability is $\frac{1}{10}$ .
18. 2 out of 10 outcomes are an even number and a head.
P(even no. & head) = $\frac{2}{10}$ = $\frac{1}{5}$  The probability is $\frac{1}{5}$ .
19. 3 out of 10 outcomes are an odd number and a tail.
P(odd no. & tail) = $\frac{3}{10}$  The probability is $\frac{3}{10}$ .
20. 1 out of 10 outcomes is a 1 and a head.
P(1 & head) = $\frac{1}{10}$  The probability is $\frac{1}{10}$ .
21. No, he is wrong.  The probability of getting a 1 and a head does not depend on any previous tries.  Sally will have the same probability to win as before.

**22.**

| | | |
|---|---|---|
| 1 | 2 | (1, 2) |
| | 3 | (1, 3) |
| | 4 | (1, 4) |
| | 5 | (1, 5) |
| 2 | 1 | (2, 1) |
| | 3 | (2, 3) |
| | 4 | (2, 4) |
| | 5 | (2, 5) |
| 3 | 1 | (3, 1) |
| | 2 | (3, 2) |
| | 4 | (3, 4) |
| | 5 | (3, 5) |
| 4 | 1 | (4, 1) |
| | 2 | (4, 2) |
| | 3 | (4, 3) |
| | 5 | (4, 5) |
| 5 | 1 | (5, 1) |
| | 2 | (5, 2) |
| | 3 | (5, 3) |
| | 4 | (5, 4) |

**23.** There are 20 possible outcomes.

**24.** Yes.

**25.** 2 out of 20 outcomes are even numbers.

P(even nos.) = $\frac{2}{20}$ = $\frac{1}{10}$

The probability is $\frac{1}{10}$ .

**26.** 12 out of 20 outcomes are 6 or more.

P(6 or >6) = $\frac{12}{20}$ = $\frac{3}{5}$

The probability is $\frac{3}{5}$ .

**27.** 0 out of 20 outcomes is 1.

P(1) = 0    The probability is 0.

**28.** 0 out of 20 outcomes is having 2 cards of the same number.

P(same no.) = 0

The probability is 0.

### Challenge

Spinner 1 : P(A) = $\frac{1}{3}$    P(B) = $\frac{1}{6}$    P(C) = $\frac{1}{2}$

Spinner 2 : P(A) = $\frac{1}{6}$    P(B) = $\frac{1}{3}$    P(C) = $\frac{1}{2}$

Spinner 3 : P(A) = $\frac{1}{4}$    P(B) = $\frac{1}{3}$    P(C) = $\frac{5}{12}$

Joan spun :    9 out of 60 times on A → P(A) = $\frac{9}{60}$ ≈ $\frac{1}{6}$

19 out of 60 times on B → P(B) = $\frac{19}{60}$ ≈ $\frac{1}{3}$

32 out of 60 times on C → P(C) = $\frac{32}{60}$ ≈ $\frac{1}{2}$

Joan spun spinner 2.

### Final Review

1. No. of toothbrushes : 35000 + 45000 + 65000 = 145000
   145 000 toothbrushes were produced in the 1st quarter.

2. No. of toothbrushes : 15000 + 40000 + 60000 = 115000
   115 000 toothbrushes were produced in the 3rd quarter.

3. Difference : (10000 + 50000 + 70000) – (25000 + 35000 + 50000)
   = 20000
   20 000 more toothbrushes were produced in the 4th quarter.

4. Amount collected : (145000 + 110000 + 115000 + 130000) x 0.53
   = 265000
   He would have collected $265 000.00.

5. The number of toothbrushes produced dropped sharply in the 2nd quarter and then gradually rose in the 3rd and 4th quarters.

6. The number of toothbrushes produced dropped continuously from the 1st quarter to the 4th quarter.

7. It would be machine C because it had the lowest production.

8-9.

**Locations of Stores**

a.  (2, 4)
b.  (0, 4)
c.  (6, 3)
d.  (11, 3)
e.  (9, 12)
f.  (1, 9)

10. Time : 1 h 46 min + 3 h 35 min = 5 h 21 min
    He finished his job at 5:21 p.m.

11. Time taken : 18.9 ÷ 60 = 0.315
    He would take 0.315 h (18.9 min).

12.

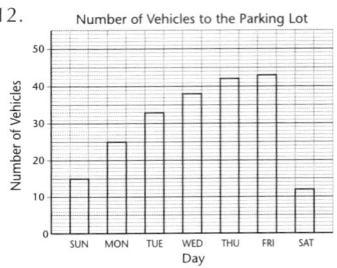

Number of Vehicles to the Parking Lot

13. More cars enter the parking lot on weekdays than on weekend.

14. Suggested answer:  It was because a lot of people did not need to go to work on Saturday and Sunday.

15. Median : 12, 15, 25, ⑨33⑩ 38, 42, 43    The median number was 33.

16. Fraction : $\frac{14}{42}$ = $\frac{1}{3}$

$\frac{1}{3}$ of vehicles were vans.

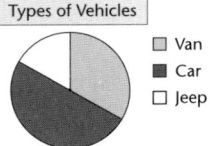

**Types of Vehicles**
- Van
- Car
- Jeep

17. 14 out of 42 vehicles were vans.

P(vans) = $\frac{14}{42}$ = $\frac{1}{3}$    The probability would be $\frac{1}{3}$ .

18.

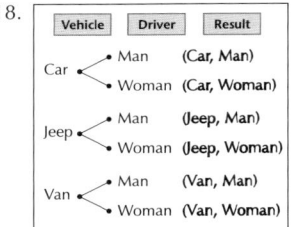

| Vehicle | Driver | Result |
|---|---|---|
| Car | Man | (Car, Man) |
| | Woman | (Car, Woman) |
| Jeep | Man | (Jeep, Man) |
| | Woman | (Jeep, Woman) |
| Van | Man | (Van, Man) |
| | Woman | (Van, Woman) |

19. P(Jeep & man) = $\frac{1}{6}$
    The probability would be $\frac{1}{6}$ .

20. There were 10 possible outcomes.  There were 3 out of 10 chances that a female driver came to pick up her car.
    The probability would be $\frac{3}{10}$ .

21. Width : 612 ÷ 25.5 = 24
    Its width is 24 m.

22. Area : (612 – (612 ÷ 3)) ÷ (3.4 x 2) = 60
    There will be 60 parking spaces.

23. Perimeter : (25.5 + 24) x 2 = 99    The perimeter is 99 m.

24. a. Signs A, B and E are the rotation images of the shaded sign.
    b. Signs D and F are the reflection images of the shaded sign.

25. Paid by hours : 3.25 + 2.15 x 6 = 16.15    (16.15 < 18)
    It would not be wise to buy a whole day ticket.

26. C          27. B          28. B          29. A

30. D          31. A          32. C